EMPERORS OF THE ICE

EMPERORS OF THE ICE

A TRUE STORY of DISASTER and SURVIVAL in the ANTARCTIC, 1910–13

Richard Farr

Farrar, Straus and Giroux
New York

Distributed in Canada by Douglas & McIntyre Ltd.
Printed in the United States of America
Designed by Robbin Gourley and Irene Metaxatos
First edition, 2008
10   9   8   7   6   5   4   3   2   1

Illustration credits appear on page 214.

www.fsgkidsbooks.com

Library of Congress Cataloging-in-Publication Data
Farr, Richard (Richard Alan Reynard), date.
    Emperors of the ice : a true story of disaster and survival in the Antarctic, 1910–13 /
Richard Farr.— 1st ed.
        p.   cm.
    Summary: Apsley "Cherry" Cherry-Garrard shares his adventures as the youngest member of
Robert Scott's expedition to Antarctica in the early twentieth century, during which he
and Edward Wilson try to learn the evolutionary history of emperor penguins. Includes
historical notes.
        ISBN-13: 978-0-374-31975-5
        ISBN-10: 0-374-31975-8
        1. British Antarctic ("Terra Nova") Expedition (1910–1913)—Juvenile fiction.   2.
Cherry-Garrard, Apsley, 1886–1959—Juvenile fiction.   3. Wilson, Edward Adrian,
1874–1912—Juvenile fiction.   4. Scott, Robert Falcon, 1868–1912—Juvenile fiction.   [1.
British Antarctic ("Terra Nova") Expedition (1910–1913)—Fiction.   2. Cherry-Garrard,
Apsley, 1886–1959—Fiction.   3. Wilson, Edward Adrian, 1872–1912—Fiction.   4. Scott, Robert
Falcon, 1868–1912—Fiction.   5. Explorers—Fiction.   6. Emperor penguin—Fiction.   7.
Penguins—Fiction.   8. Antarctica—Discovery and exploration—Fiction.]   I. Title.

PZ7.F2405Emp 2008
[Fic]—dc22
                                                                                    2007052347

In memoriam

Dr. Edward A. Wilson, 1872–1912
Lieutenant Henry R. Bowers, 1883–1912
Apsley G. B. Cherry-Garrard, 1886–1959

I cannot rest from travel: I will drink
Life to the lees . . . —Tennyson, "Ulysses"

This winter travel is a new and bold venture,
but the right men have gone to attempt it.

—Robert Falcon Scott, *Journals*

Take it all in all, I do not believe anybody
on earth has a worse time than an Emperor penguin.

—Apsley Cherry-Garrard,
The Worst Journey in the World

The past is a foreign country:
they do things differently there.

—L. P. Hartley, *The Go-Between*

CONTENTS

MAPS

CHARTS

PREFACE

ANTARCTIC EXPLORATION IS seldom as bad as you imagine . . . But this journey had beggared our language: no words could express its horror." Thus did Apsley Cherry-Garrard describe the "Winter Journey" that he undertook, with the two best friends he would ever have, in 1911. It's an almost literally incredible story.

A.C.G. in Antarctica: No skill that could be of the slightest use during a blizzard on an ice-floe

"Cherry" left England for Antarctica with Robert Falcon Scott in the spring of 1910 and returned home to the family estate in Hertfordshire nearly three years later. He took nearly ten years to finish writing about his Polar experiences, and the manuscript ran to a quarter of a million words, covering in detail almost every aspect of Scott's great, multifaceted expedition.

It helped that his neighbor and close friend, half a mile across the fields at Ayot St. Lawrence, was the playwright George Bernard Shaw. Shaw took a keen interest in the project, did some editing, and suggested that a phrase Cherry used—"the worst journey in the world!"—would do nicely for a title. But the real achievement of Cherry's book is its spirit, and that is all his own: a deep love of life, a boyish delight in adventure and the overcoming of hardship, and a kind of gourmet appreciation for the constitutions of exceptional men.

Published in 1922, *The Worst Journey in the World* may be the best volume of exploration literature ever written. I read it many years ago, and loved it so much that I yacked on about it at length to anyone who would listen. But eventually it occurred to me that most of these people, however much they nodded and smiled, would not get around to reading such a doorstop. Besides, there were hundreds of books about Scott's tragic retreat from the South Pole, and what inspired me most was not the Polar story so much as Cherry's own. The Winter Journey: the mad jaunt, the mind-bogglingly hellish side-expedition, that he undertook along with Bill Wilson and Birdie Bowers, all for a chance to study the eggs of the Emperor penguin.

Briefly, I harbored the illusion that doing this would be easy. I would write a short, simple history book, a third-person snapshot of the Winter Journey that left out everything else.

Unfortunately, it's hard to leave out anything at all. The mass of detail in Cherry's book underlines a point that's important for understanding the Winter Journey itself. Scott did not, as people commonly think, take one expedition to the South Pole in 1910. He took *half a dozen* expeditions, all in the one ship, to *Antarctica*. Each expedition was designed to explore, in the cause of science, a different aspect of an unknown continent. Marine biology in McMurdo Sound. Geology and glaciation in the Western Mountains. The atmosphere. The magnetic field. Parasitology.

And bird evolution. That special interest was the only reason Scott's chief scientist, Bill Wilson, had agreed to join the expedition. People remember a race to the Pole, but even Scott was more interested in his scientists' search for new knowledge. As for Wilson, he didn't give a hoot about flag-waving. He was in the South because he loved God's creation and wanted to understand it better. His motive for planning and leading a near-suicidal bid to find some unusual birds' eggs was not national pride, but the desire to honor a gloriously unlikely pair of personal heroes, St. Francis of Assisi and Charles Darwin.

In the end, I did have to leave out most of the science. By doing so, I also left out one other side-expedition that turned as memorably ghastly as the Winter Journey.* On the other hand, not telling the main Polar story really was impossible. As you will see, Cherry's connection to that tragedy was so acutely personal that it colored everything else in his life, including his memories.

But I had worse problems than what to omit. I kept finding material that was directly relevant, yet missing even from Cherry's great compendium of facts. And, as the extra details piled up, it became clear that something else was missing, too:

---

*Victor Campbell led the "Northern Party," investigating the geography, geology, and fauna of Victoria Land, to the north and east of Scott's base in McMurdo Sound. The six men were unexpectedly trapped for the whole winter of 1912 when sea ice made it impossible to pick them up. They should have died from exposure or starvation; instead they dug a tiny ice cave and survived by eating such delicacies as half-digested fish that they found in the bellies of the few seals they were able to kill. Despite scurvy and dysentery, none of them died. None of them even went insane, though it was close. The following spring, presumed dead, they dug themselves out and sledged the 230 miles "home."

dialogue. Whispered conversations began to float off every new document I read; I found myself shuffling closer, eavesdropping, and scribbling down what I thought these men were saying to one another.

Soon, despite a desk overflowing with notes and drafts, I had no idea how to proceed. So I took a break and picked up Beryl Bainbridge's novel *The Birthday Boys*. It was a revelation. There are five chapters, each narrated by one of the men who died on Scott's final march. Bainbridge puts you inside their heads. By the time I put down her book, I knew that mine could no longer be a straightforward history. Sure, I needed the historian's benefit of hindsight; I also needed the novelist's benefit of insight. I would have to tell Cherry's story in his own voice, as he had done, but I would have to use dialogue too, really *imagine* these men—and in a strange way reinvent Cherry himself.

The Cherry of 1922 was thorough, wrote beautifully, and tried hard to be objective. His book is indispensable because, even though the main facts can be found in other sources— sometimes only in other sources—*Worst Journey* is where we discover what Cherry thought and felt. In a very few places I have even used his exact words, because they constitute a fact about him, or almost his exact words, because some phrase seemed irreplaceable.* In short, it would have been impossi-

---

*See, for example, the mantra in Chapter 7, the last two sentences of that chapter, and the "pure shining gold" remark in Chapter 9. You will also see quotation marks in a couple of the photo captions: these indicate Cherry's words direct from *Worst Journey*. From time to time I have recycled choice words from other sources, too: what I imagine Trigger Gran says to Cherry in Chapter 9 is taken, almost but not quite verbatim, from Gran's diary.

ble to write my book without his. Yet Cherry wrote in the grip of strange passions that distorted his judgment. I even found points on which I concluded that *Worst Journey* was simply wrong.* So I had to compromise. "My" Cherry writes what I believe he *would* have written had he been able to put certain obsessions aside, absorb the arguments that have continued to rage over the expedition to this day, and consider all evidence and all sources from the viewpoint of our own time.

You might conclude that the result in your hands is a strange creature indeed—a fictional memoir for which the key source is a real memoir. But permit me to protest: this book is not fiction. Consider the analogy of how best to restore an old painting. Fiction is a bag of tools; I use them here to fill, as authentically and consistently as possible, the gaps on a historical canvas. At every point, I have tried to let the known facts guide me. At every point, my aim has been, like Cherry's, to paint a true picture of the past.

⬤⬤⬤

Speaking of the past, it's important to understand that these events took place before the Great War of 1914–18. We are taught today that digital technology is pretty important, or in-

---

*Soon after it was published, Cherry received an anguished letter from Sidney Harmer, Director of London's Natural History Museum. In a press interview, and then in *Worst Journey*, Cherry described being mistreated by Museum staff in July 1913. Harmer believed Cherry's version was a slanderous fiction. A careful reading of the primary sources convinced me that Harmer was right. Cherry's version makes for a good after-dinner anecdote, but it is not honest. You will find my version—what I think actually happened—in Chapter 9.

ternational terrorism, or global warming. But the impact of all these things has been trivial, so far at least, compared to the Great War, a conflict whose scale and savagery divide all before it from all after it like a great Rift Valley across the plain of time. Because of the Great War, the gulf separating us from the early twentieth century is even wider than "a hundred years" suggests. It can be difficult enough to reach beyond the obvious things—the funny clothes, the stiff manners, the quaint assumptions—to grasp what these men were like as individuals. When we succeed, it can be harder still to believe how familiar, and at the same time how different from us, they seem.

E. P. Thompson famously said that the business of the historian is to rescue the past "from the enormous condescension of posterity." What he meant, I think, is that we owe it to the dead to take them as seriously as we take ourselves. Yet there are two sides to this metaphor of rescue. Scott and his men had something precious that we have lost. *Worst Journey* describes superhuman feats of courage and endurance. Above all, though, it describes men who performed these feats quietly, with a sense of humor, and without a shred of either self-pity or self-importance. That extraordinary spirit is what makes Cherry's book such a thrilling read. I hope I have captured a little of it in these lesser pages.

One day, perhaps, you will turn to *Worst Journey* itself, and then you can compare the words I have put in Cherry's mouth, based on all the evidence in front of me, with what he wrote. But in case you never do, here is his final paragraph, which offers you his prejudices and values in a nutshell:

And I tell you, if you have the desire for knowledge and the power to give it physical expression, go out and explore. If you are a brave man you will do nothing: if you are fearful you may do much, for none but cowards have need to prove their bravery. Some will tell you that you are mad, and nearly all will say, "What is the use?" For we are a nation of shopkeepers, and no shopkeeper will look at research which does not promise him a financial return within a year. And so you will sledge nearly alone, but those with whom you sledge will not be shopkeepers: that is worth a good deal. If you march your Winter Journeys you will have your reward, so long as all you want is a penguin's egg.

Cherry did not literally mean "shopkeepers," of course: he meant "people for whom all value is money value." He might have been talking about us: our "enormous condescension" to the past shows up with embarrassing clarity both in the way we have learned to sneer at the Edwardian cult of the amateur and in the powerful cult we have built, instead, around the word *professional*. A professional, Cherry would have said, is simply a highly paid subspecies of shopkeeper. And what he tells us about friendship, the raw desire for knowledge, and selfless determination in the face of impossible odds is a heart-stopping reminder of what the word *amateur* actually means.

EMPERORS OF THE ICE

1

LUCKIEST MAN ALIVE

LONDON TO NEW ZEALAND,
APRIL TO DECEMBER 1910

SANDWICHES AND GAMES. Slices of cake and patches of winter sunlight. Presents in bright ribbons from my sisters. At a house in the English countryside, on the second day of the twentieth century, I am celebrating my fourteenth birthday.

But I don't remember celebrating. What I remember is sitting alone in the drawing room, paging through a new atlas with a bright red cover, and accepting glumly that I had been born too late.

The stories were all there, illustrated in color, with maps and arrows. Louis-Antoine de Bougainville charting the South Seas. John Hanning Speke, David Livingstone, and Mungo Park opening the African interior to European knowledge. Sir Richard Burton "doing" Arabia, the remoter parts of India, and much else besides. Edward Whymper conquering the unconquerable Matterhorn. Captain Cook sailing around the world—and then doing it twice more, as if to rub in the fact

A.C.G.'s rowing team, Christ Church 2nd Torpid, Oxford, 1906

that he was a better navigator, and more daring, and had seen more and had more fun, than any man before or since.

It seemed there was nowhere left to explore, though there were just a few places, if you looked closely. You would win lasting fame if you found the fabled Northwest Passage between the Atlantic and Pacific Oceans! But, when I and the new century were still young, the great Norwegian Roald Amundsen, sailing his tiny herring boat *Gjøa*, did just that. What about the North Pole? You would be immortal if you were the first man there! Only three years after Amundsen's incredible news, when I was still a young man, the American Robert Peary knocked that one off the list, too.

Of course, if you wanted to go somewhere *unknown*, there was still one place left. Just one. The great white blank at the bottom of the map.

Antarctica!

And how unknown it was. Men had been going north to explore the Arctic since the time of the Vikings, but mad King George was already dead and coal gas lit the cities of his realm by the time a human eye first traced the Antarctic coastline.* A whole succession of expeditions proceeded to paw feebly at the fringes of this new world, establishing that there was a continent and not just a frozen archipelago waiting. Then two

---

*Or very nearly dead. The first man to see Antarctica was probably Fabian Gottlieb von Bellingshausen, on Friday, 28 January 1820, aboard the *Vostok*. The very next day, merciful death finally claimed George III at Windsor Castle; the day after *that*, Edward Bransfield of the Royal Navy saw the new continent for the first time, landed on a nearby island, and named it after the man he incorrectly believed was still his king.

British expeditions, by Robert Falcon Scott and Ernest Shackleton, came agonisingly close to planting a flag at the South Pole. In 1902, reaching a point within 500 miles made Scott famous. In 1909, a closer mark, less than 100 miles short of the goal, made Shackleton so famous that he rated an effigy, complete with sledge and Polar clothing, at Madame Tussaud's waxwork museum in London.

Robert Falcon Scott. The official Navy portrait

Still, when in September 1909 Scott announced that he would make a second attempt to reach the South Pole, even he must have been surprised by the response.

He had already picked most of his ship's crew: he was a Navy officer, after all. He had also picked many of the men who would form the Shore Party. He just needed a few specialists, mostly scientists. If they were fit, hard-working men with the right qualifications, he was offering a job like no other. Two years of fearsomely hard work, poorly paid, with extreme discomfort and constant danger of death, in the remotest wasteland on the face of the planet.

Eight thousand people applied.

Was this Captain Scott's reputation at work, or just the drug-like allure of going to the last place of all? A bit of both, I suppose. At all events, the letters and telegrams flooded in from every corner of the British Empire. Eager volunteers clamoured to join this heroic enterprise, even offering large sums of their own money for the privilege. Geologists from Scotland. Mine engineers from Africa. Soldiers from India. Adventurers, dreamers, and lunatics from all points of the compass—and, mostly from England, a smattering of people like me.

In 1909 I was no longer a boy, but I might as well have been. A wealthy young gentleman aged twenty-three, I had no special talent, no relevant experience, and no useful expertise. I had forgotten, more or less, my dreams of becoming an explorer, but I was powerfully bored with my country house and my comfort. Hearing Scott's plans, I was thrilled to think that I might be included in an undertaking so brave and strange.

Scott got his top-notch scientists. The meteorologist George Simpson. The surgeon and parasitologist Edward Atkinson. The Canadian physicist Charles "Silas" Wright. The Australian geologists Frank Debenham and Griffith Taylor. So how the dickens did I (Mr. Apsley George Benet Cherry-Garrard, but please, please call me Cherry) manage to get myself accepted into this company?

A good question.

I had recently graduated from Oxford, where I had an absolutely super time and learned nothing. I was not a scientist, and I had no skill that could be of the slightest use during a blizzard on an ice-floe. Even before I knew about the eight thousand others, I rated my chances poorly. All I had was a connection.

A year earlier, on holiday in Scotland, I had met a tall,

mild-mannered young doctor named Edward Wilson. "Uncle Bill," as I came to know him, was investigating diseases in game birds, an occupation that suited his brilliant scientific mind, love of nature, and thirst for physical exercise. The same could be said of his previous job. He had travelled south as Scott's Assistant Surgeon aboard the *Discovery*; on 31 December 1902, he had stood with Scott and Shackleton at their "farthest south," just 480 miles from the Pole.*

For the new adventure, naturally, Wilson was not one of the eight thousand hopefuls: Scott had already seen enough to judge that he was "the best fellow that ever stepped" and had asked him to become his Chief Scientific Officer. It was Uncle Bill, standing on a heather-covered hill with an injured grouse in one hand and his pipe in the other, who told me (shortly before it was known by everyone else in Christendom) that Scott would be going to Antarctica again.

I applied, offering the expedition a generous donation, and was not in the least surprised to be rejected. On a whim, perhaps because I felt that supporting the expedition would be a little bit like going anyway, I wrote to Scott saying that I understood perfectly and he could keep the money. He liked the gesture enough to mention it to Bill. Bill grasped the opportunity to say flattering things about me. Scott suddenly suggested that we meet after all.

---

*The Pole, of course, marks exactly 90° South. In 1902, Scott, Shackleton, and Wilson turned back at latitude 82°17' South. In 1908, Shackleton went to Antarctica again aboard the *Nimrod*, without Scott this time; his team made it to 88°23' South. See map, p. 25.

Bill was probably wise to splash cold water on my glow of excitement: "Don't get your hopes up, Cherry," he said. "Captain Scott just wants to be polite. As for a place on the expedition, it does not look promising at all. Be at his office on Wednesday at eleven o'clock."

And so it was that on 27 April 1910, just five weeks before the expedition was due to leave, I took an early morning train up to London for an interview. A hansom cab deposited me outside the capital's most recent homage to modern architecture, Westminster Cathedral—a brick monstrosity that looks more like a railway station than a place of worship. Across the way, at 36 Victoria Street, I found an office building with a small sign tacked to the door: BRITISH ANTARCTIC EXPEDITION, 1910. I waited in the hallway for several minutes, eyeing my watch for the precise hour. It was then that I caught the first whiff of Scott's pungent pipe tobacco.

My timid knock was answered with a brief, barked "Enter!" A second later I was standing before a neat, powerful man who seemed every inch the officer even in his dark civilian suit. The room he presided over, however, was a poorly lit office containing two shabby wooden desks, an explosion of nautical charts, and several Venesta cases* that seemed to have vomited up large quantities of brass scientific equipment.

I found myself stammering an introduction. I was nervous

The font in the right margin reads: *The best fellow that ever stepped: Dr. Edward Adrian Wilson*

---

*The Venesta Plywood Company produced a strong, waterproof, and lightweight plywood, from which most of the expedition's crates were made. The name comes from combining the word *veneer* with the company's country of origin, *Estonia*.

despite telling myself that the whole conversation would consist of him saying "Jolly decent of you about the money" and me saying "Don't even think of it. I do wish you the best of luck!" As it turned out, he never mentioned money at all, and his first words were:

"Dr. Wilson says you are still quite interested in coming to Antarctica."

I think I actually laughed. Quite interested! It was my first introduction to Scott's great gift for understatement. Just imagine being the only man in the world who is selling tickets to the only destination in the world that almost no one has ever visited. He understood perfectly well that, like most of his volunteers, I would have walked barefoot to Antarctica across broken glass if that had been among his requirements.

Perhaps he read my thoughts, and saw the image that had floated through my mind: Cherry and Scott, plus Wilson, standing on the ice next to a victory flag. Or perhaps he simply guessed that I had read the expedition's new pamphlet, with its grand introduction: "The main object of this Expedition is to reach the South Pole, and to secure for the British Empire the honour of that achievement."

Scott put me straight about that immediately. "Look," he continued, in his pleasant but direct way, "you need to understand from the start what this expedition is about. I have two quite distinct goals. The South Pole, yes. Of course, the Pole, which I want to claim before the Americans or the Norwegians get there. That is what the newspapers and the public will be obsessed with: the Union Flag fluttering at ninety degrees south, glory for Old England and all that business.

Aside from anything else, I could not raise a penny without telling everyone ad nauseam that we will conquer the Pole. But it's window-dressing, to be frank. The Pole is a single meaningless point that happens to lie at the centre of our ignorance—five million square miles of ignorance. My own motivation is to discover a continent, not a point, and to do the kind of science that will put that continent on the map. I want experiments, detailed logs of detailed observations, new knowledge. A whole research program. Geology. Zoology. Magnetics. Radio-activity. Topography. Climate. Bathymetry."

I nodded and made a mental note to look up *bathymetry* as soon as I got home. It sounded like another item in a long list of reasons he would not choose a man like me. "I'm not surprised by your emphasis on science," I said. "Dr. Wilson made that very clear to me when he told me about the penguin business."

Missing link?
Sketch by Bill of an
Emperor penguin

"Ah, yes! Dear Bill is quite obsessed with his penguins. He thinks they're a sort of missing link between birds and dinosaurs." He grinned. "Perhaps he's right!"

Bill had told me, up there on the grouse moor, about the penguins. "Emperors, the biggest of their kind." Along with Charles Royds and Reginald Skelton, on Scott's *Discovery*, he had investigated a remote breeding colony; now he wanted to visit it again, in the winter, to test a theory about the evolution of birds. "The basic idea is very simple," he had said. "The dinosaurs didn't become extinct. Or not all of them. Dinosaurs are all around us. Just very small, feathery, flying ones." He laughed, as if admitting the idea was absurd, but I knew at once that he meant it. "A bird's whole skeleton looks like a dinosaur's, especially the skull. There's absolutely no chance it's a coincidence, if you ask me. I also think that the Emperor may be the most primitive bird of all, perhaps a direct descendant of some Jurassic reptile like *Archaeopteryx*. If we could take a closer look at its eggs . . ."

That morning in London, though, I was not concerned with penguins and had no way of knowing that a four-foot variety with strange breeding habits would be the cause of the most memorable and most nearly lethal adventure in my life. Standing in that office, very self-conscious and feeling that I was a hopelessly inadequate specimen of my own species, I was concerned only with how I must look in the eyes of Captain Scott. What did I have to offer, after all? I was ten years younger than most of his men. My genuine interest in science could neither mask nor make up for my ignorance. As for physical ability: I was a rower, which had made me fit, but I had only taken up rowing because it was the one sport in which being shortsighted didn't matter. Rowing at Oxford meant sitting on the nice calm river and slicing backwards through the dawn mist while the coxswain, the little man facing forward from the stern, bleated instructions. Most pleasant, and I recommend it highly. Especially for someone like me, whose eyesight is so bad that without my glasses I could make a life-threatening expedition out of climbing the main staircase at the Ritz Hotel.

It's a funny thing, how men make decisions. They line up all the evidence, get it all on paper. They weigh, calculate, consider. Then they ignore the evidence and go with their gut. I liked Scott at once; apparently, he liked me at once. We finished our conversation by talking about horses, a detail I remember because I know a fair bit about horses and it turned out that Scott should perhaps have known more than he did. Shortly after our meeting, apparently, he muttered something to Uncle Bill about "needing a general helper" and how I would "undoubtedly prove useful." Against all the odds, I was a member of the team.

The month that followed was like a dream: feverish preparation for an exotic two-year holiday that I could not quite believe I would be allowed to go on. I ordered clothes and equipment, sent them back or had them adjusted, and tried to beat the rudiments of celestial navigation into my head. Since it is assumed that a man of my background will never have to prepare a meal in his life, I even had to demand of our family cook, who thought the whole thing most peculiar, that she teach me the mysterious arts by which dishes like porridge or boiled eggs get from the larder to the table.

The worst moment of every day was the postman's arrival. Every time I heard the crunch of his bicycle on the gravel, I was sure there would be a letter from Wilson explaining that the whole thing was a mistake. I opened that letter a thousand times in my head: "Dear Cherry, Awfully sorry to be the bearer of bad tidings. Scott has decided he simply must take so-and-so in your place." But the days passed and the letter did not arrive.

Each evening, briefly relieved of such anxieties and snug in my favourite chair, I dug my way down through a stack of books, trying to uncover every known scrap of information about Antarctica, including everything Scott and Wilson had written about their *Discovery* expedition. As I soon learned, that expedition had been driven by the same two goals. Closeness to the Pole was what the public remembered, but the men had also done plenty of geologising and had returned with thick stacks of notes on animal life and the weather. Bill Wilson was especially proud of that.

Scott was shopping, of course, just as I was. He had already been to Norway to buy reindeer-skin bags and wolf-skin mittens, and while there he also acquired the services of Tryggve "Trigger" Gran, an impressive skier.*

He had also bought the largest item on his list, the elderly Dundee whaling ship *Terra Nova*. Built in 1884, she had three masts and a single yellow funnel attached to coal-fired boilers that were already old-fashioned. She would be going to Antarctica for the second time. In 1903, after Scott's first ship, *Discovery*, became trapped in the coastal ice, the Admiralty

---

*In 1890, when Fridtjof Nansen wrote *The First Crossing of Greenland*, skiing was virtually unknown outside Scandinavia. The long wooden planks were thought of as skinny snowshoes: a *skilöber* is literally a "snow runner." Members of Scott's expedition followed the Norwegians in referring to "ski" rather than "skis"—and pronouncing the word, as Nansen himself put it, exactly like the English *she*. (Thus: "A party of four men on *she* came up to the hut.") The Norwegian *skilöbers* usually propelled themselves with a single long pole, though by 1910 the modern pair of sticks was increasingly common. Scott met the expert skier Tryggve Gran when he went to Norway to test equipment. Although only twenty, Gran was already planning his own Antarctic expedition; Scott invited him to join the British expedition instead. Under Gran's tutelage, Scott's men generally used a pair of sticks, but they experimented with both styles.

sent the *Morning* and the *Terra Nova* to "rescue" her crew. The *Terra Nova*
Scott was furious. He was prepared to spend another winter
in Antarctica anyway, did not like the British public getting the
false impression that he needed rescuing, and was disgusted
by the thought of abandoning the *Discovery*. Well, the winter
ice hung on grimly until the last moment but gave up its grip
just soon enough for Scott to ignore his orders.

Scott's fame had not made him rich. By 1909, the *Discovery* was no longer his and the *Terra Nova* was what he could
afford. She reeked of whale-oil and had been so poorly maintained that one couldn't quite tell whether she was black from
paint or from grease. She should perhaps have been allowed
to rot out her retirement at some gull-smeared quay in England. Instead, Scott paid for half of her, promised the rest

The Men of the *Terra Nova* Expedition

* Captain Robert Falcon Scott, Royal Navy

† Lieutenant E. R. G. R. "Teddy" Evans, Royal Navy, Second in
   Command of the *Terra Nova*

* Dr. Edward Adrian "Uncle Bill" Wilson, doctor, Chief of Scientific
   Staff, and Zoologist

* Captain Lawrence E. G. "Titus" Oates, 6th Inniskilling Dragoons
   (Army), in charge of ponies

* Lieutenant Henry Robertson "Birdie" Bowers, Royal Indian Marines,
   in charge of stores

* Petty Officer Edgar "Taff" Evans, Royal Navy

   Apsley G. B. "Cherry" Cherry-Garrard, Assistant Zoologist

   Edward L. "Atch" Atkinson, Royal Navy Surgeon, parasitologist

   Charles S. "Silas" Wright (Canadian), physicist

   Tryggve "Trigger" Gran (Norwegian), ski instructor

   Chief Stoker William Lashly, Royal Navy

   Petty Officer Tom Crean, Royal Navy

   Petty Officer Patrick Keohane, Royal Navy

   Dimitri S. Gerof (Russian), dog-handler

   Lieutenant Victor L. A. "The Wicked Mate" Campbell, Royal Navy

† Thomas Griffith "Griff" Taylor (Australian), geologist

† Herbert G. "Ponko" Ponting, Camera Artist

† Cecil H. Meares, a much-travelled private adventurer, in charge
of dogs

† Thomas C. Clissold, Royal Navy, cook

Frank "Deb" Debenham (Australian), geologist

Frederick J. Hooper, Royal Navy, steward

† George C. "Sunny Jim" Simpson, meteorologist

Edward W. "Marie" Nelson, biologist

Petty Officer George P. Abbott, Royal Navy

Petty Officer Frank V. Browning, Royal Navy

Able Seaman Harry Dickason, Royal Navy

George M. "Toffer" Levick, Royal Navy, Surgeon

Raymond E. "Ray" Priestley, geographer

† Petty Officer Robert Forde, Royal Navy

† Bernard C. Day, motor sledge engineer

† Anton Omelchenko (Russian), groom

Died on the expedition
†*Returned to New Zealand in 1911*

Chief Steward W. Archer and Petty Officer Thomas S. Williamson came down with the *Terra Nova* in 1911 and joined the Shore Party. Thomas Clissold had to be replaced, having injured his back falling from an iceberg during a Ponting photographic session. Several other men, including Ponting and Taylor, also returned to civilisation. This left a total of thirteen men at Cape Evans to face the second winter. In addition to the men listed here, over thirty Navy officers, Navy ratings, and scientific staff remained on the *Terra Nova* during the expedition but were not part of the Shore Party.

(without the ghost of an idea where "the rest" was coming from), and had her cleaned. Then, with volunteer labour, he began the long and difficult business of reconfiguring her for two to three years in the Antarctic.

We sailed from Cardiff, which had donated a large amount of coal, on 15 June 1910.* Scott himself was among the crowd waving from shore, because he had to spend more time in London, raising funds. He would meet us that autumn in South Africa.

❥❥❥

There was much to do during the long months at sea, but it was a happy and carefree time. Although I was seasick every time it got rough, which was frequently, I took comfort from the fact that some of the other "landsmen" got it even worse than I did. As the weather grew warmer, I loved being on deck in the open air, mending equipment or netting marine specimens or just shifting crates of supplies.

Many years later, I was to learn something else about this time. Bill Wilson was writing about me in his diary. What a good choice I had been! Cheerful, hard-working, "invaluable," et cetera, et cetera. Scott himself must have received reports of me along the same lines. After he rejoined us in South Africa, he wrote that I had "won all hearts."

Perhaps I was lucky not to hear such praise at the time and

---

*Cardiff was the port to which the *Terra Nova* returned at the end of the expedition, almost exactly three years later—on 14 June 1913.

run the risk of thinking too well of myself. I was so busy and so excited by the constant parade of new experiences that the idea of my activities being "work" never entered my head. My only care was that others on board might resent my youth, my lack of knowledge, my inexperience.

Yet I could not let even this bother me much. For the first time in my life, I was neither doing what duty and custom demanded at home nor idly playing the tourist abroad. I had escaped everyday life and committed myself to a grand adventure. Antarctica was a long way off: the nagging thought—*will I be tough enough?*—stayed out of sight, mostly, at the back of my mind. Working twelve hours a day, dark brown from the sun, and covered in salt spray, I considered myself the luckiest man alive.

2

DYING TO GET THERE

SOUTHERN OCEAN, DECEMBER 1910

AFTER BRIEFLY STRETCHING our legs in South Africa, where Scott joined us as planned, and then again in Australia, we spent a whole month in preparation on New Zealand's green, beautiful South Island. It seemed ironic to me that a place of such human generosity and natural abundance was our launching-point for an expedition to an uninhabited and frozen desert. But, as we steamed out of Port Chalmers—Dunedin's main port—on 29 November 1910, with crowds waving and church bells ringing, I was reminded that getting to the frozen desert required us to cross another desert first.

As we turned south out of Otago Harbour that spring day, our latitude was already 46° South: we were in the "Roaring Forties," as generations of storm-tossed sailors have found good reason to name them. But for two pleasant days the sailing seemed routine. We got back into our rhythms of work, feeling relaxed and giving little thought to the sea. In conversation, and in the private theatre of our own imaginations, we indulged our fixation on the white continent ahead, the last

Crossing another desert first: the Terra Nova *in the Southern Ocean*

great wilderness. We left New Zealand far behind over the northern horizon, and during the early hours of Thursday, 1 December, we approached close to her lonely southern outpost, Campbell Island.

The *Terra Nova* may have been old and crowded, but we had come to love and respect her on the journey down from London. She was sturdy, as you might expect from the seven-foot thickness of oak keel designed to shrug off ice-floes, but she also handled well. A persistent leak was the worst of our complaints, and in New Zealand, Captain Scott found the ideal man to fix it. We had been based at the port of Lyttelton. By happy accident the town's mayor was also a master shipwright. He found the source of the leak—a bolt in the stern that was too small for the bolt hole. Although it proved impossible to cure the leak totally, he reduced it to a trickle we could manage.

The rest of us had spent much of our time in New Zealand doing something quite else to the *Terra Nova*: loading her, loading her, loading her. She needed eight tons of coal a day under full steam, so we squeezed 462 tons of the stuff into her hold. Then we added so much food, animal fodder, and equipment that she was low in the water before we even started packing the decks.

Topside, we built extra animal stalls, and a zinc-lined ice-house that was to hold 162 mutton carcases, three beef carcases, various other perishables, and three tons of ice.*

---

*The ice-house was not a complete success: some of the meat was already rotting by the time it reached Antarctica. Scott was criticised later for hauling meat to a place where, in the form of seal, it was the one abundant resource. No such critic has ever led an expedition. Like leaders before and since, Scott took what he was given.

Next to the ice-house we lashed down three enormous wooden crates containing new-fangled aluminium motor sledges. These had been custom-built for the expedition in Birmingham by the Wolseley Tool and Motor Company, which was experimenting at the time with that exciting new invention, the motor-car. Scott took the sledges to Norway and tried them out on a frozen lake, where they did very well; they were shipped separately as far as New Zealand. Scott believed that motorised transport was the future of Polar travel; he was right about that, and his willingness to try this bold experiment made us feel thoroughly modern, thoroughly twentieth-century.

Around the crates we packed an extra thirty tons of coal, fifteen tons of pony fodder, five tons of dog biscuits, and so many cases of petrol that the deck itself became invisible and we were forced to walk to and fro on top of the cargo. Finally, somehow, into the crevices we squeezed thirty-three snarling dogs, nineteen placid Manchurian ponies, one cat, and sixty-five slightly crazed members of the species *Homo sapiens*.

All of which is to say: we left New Zealand with the *Terra Nova* seriously overloaded. On the afternoon of that first day in December, in some of the most dangerous waters on earth, we sailed her into a storm.

●●●

Below New Zealand, below Tasmania and South America and South Africa, too, the Southern Ocean encircles the earth. The winds there have no land to break their stride, and they blow without ceasing. Their work, to which they are passionately committed, is wave-building, and the waves they build are monsters: mile-long rolling peaks of slate, capped with avalanches of foam. That is in calm weather.

The first day out, I fooled myself that perhaps, at last, I was mastering the sea-sickness that had plagued me for so long, but these huge southern swells quickly unsettled my stomach and my nerves all over again. Sitting near the mizzenmast* after lunch, I was darning a pair of socks and trying not to think about whether my turtle soup would stay down, when I noticed a subtle change. The swells were shortening, their surfaces becoming rougher, and they seemed to shiver as if troubled, like me, by an invisible sickness. The spray started to get in our faces. As the air around us cooled, the deck began to make ominous groaning noises.

This went on for twenty minutes, and nothing else changed. Then, suddenly, the wind rose. The sea seemed to blacken before our eyes, as if ink were spreading up from the depths. Half-sitting and half-crouching, I grabbed the railing and looked about me in an attempt to judge whether the sailors were as alarmed by the change as I was. It was as if the ocean had transformed itself in minutes from an unruly object into a surly, malevolent *being*.

"Shorten sail!" I heard someone cry from the bow as I retched over the rail into the frothing water. The cry was re-

---

*On a three-masted barque like the *Terra Nova*, the larger foremast and mainmast were "square-rigged": they had horizontal "yards" supporting square sails. The smaller mizzenmast, or rear mast, was on the poop (rear) deck, just aft of the single funnel.

peated down the deck—"Shorten sail"..."Shorten sail"—like an echo or the sound of a gull, but the sea was too quick for us. Almost immediately, the new, more violent motion of the waves caused a cascade of problems that nearly turned our Polar expedition into the shortest on record.

Everything had seemed so carefully stowed, but it took no time at all for two coal sacks to work loose on deck. Nobody could reach them quickly, because water had started flooding through the railings and into the hold. Someone shouted at me to get down the ladder and help with bailing; by the time I had scuttled along the deck and was taking a final look around before going below, the loose sacks were crashing back and forth like a drunken boxer's gloved fists, powerful, unpredictable, indiscriminate.

We were afraid that they would knock other things loose, such as the cases of fuel. We were afraid that they would break loose entirely and injure one of the animals, or one of

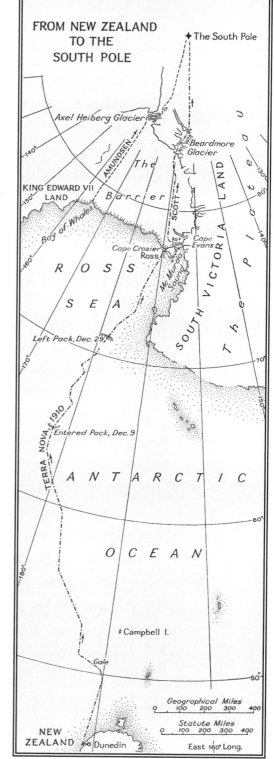

FROM NEW ZEALAND TO THE SOUTH POLE

the crew, on their way overboard. For a long time, though, the ropes held and the sacks just thudded back and forth, threatening everything and doing nothing. I was down in the stokehold, standing in two feet of oily bilge-water (I had taken down a bucket of coal and was stooping to take a bucket of water back up), when one of the coal sacks broke open and we discovered something else to worry about.

The coal dust snowed down on us, speckling the surface of the water. There it combined with the pretty sheen of leaked engine oil, and the mixture congealed into big, greasy clumps that swarmed around us like jelly-fish. To begin with, these strange aquatic creatures merely clung to our bodies. Then, as if sensing that they could cause more trouble elsewhere, they swam away to clog the bilge pumps.

The next few hours were characterised by a certain monotony. Nothing much happened, except that the wind kept rising, the waves kept growing, and, despite our frantic efforts, the water in the hold kept creeping higher. It isn't much fun standing all afternoon, and all evening, and all night, with one arm hooked around an iron ladder, freezing cold and soaking wet, hefting a slopping bucket until your shoulder muscles seem less like parts of your own body than like two abused animals squealing for mercy. But nobody made anything of his own discomfort in those terrible hours, partly because we knew that the actual animals, our own poor ponies and dogs, had it far worse than any of us. Thrown from side to side, buried for a minute at a time under the hissing water, they were almost hanged again and again by their own leads. Lawrence "Titus" Oates, the cavalry officer in charge of the

They certainly preferred him to any other human: Titus Oates on deck with the animals

ponies, fought for their safety, and his mere presence seemed to calm them. When one of them fell or was washed off its feet, he would wrap his arms around it and help it up again. I liked and respected Titus—we all did, long before he taught us how brave men choose to die—but he was a man of few words. He preferred the company of animals. They certainly preferred him to any other human.*

Alas, even Titus could not protect all of the animals from this storm. I was out on deck for a change, frantically lashing and hauling, when one of our best dogs, imperious dark-furred Osman, was hit by a wall of water that snapped his chain and washed him clear overboard. Miraculously, almost comically, the next wave washed him straight back onto the deck, where one of the men caught and re-tethered him. A

---

*On paper he was Captain Lawrence Oates, 6th Inniskilling Dragoons. His family always called him Laurie. On the expedition he was Titus, except when Scott called him Soldier because he was the only Army man, or when Birdie Bowers, making fun of his taste for dressing as scruffily as possible, addressed him as Farmer Hayseed.

second dog was not so lucky. One moment he was there, soaked and miserable but securely tied. Seconds later there was merely a space where he had been.

The darkness was brief, for this was the southern summer and the sun spent barely two hours below the horizon. Small mercies! From 2 A.M. to 4 A.M. on Friday, I had perhaps my most memorable interlude of all, taking a shift up in the sails. At that point the storm was still rising, and all I could do was cling to the yardarm and vomit from a combination of extreme sea-sickness and terror. One of our most experienced Navy men said that the wind was blowing Force 10. The biggest waves were cresting at thirty-five feet. Perhaps you will get some idea of how I felt if you try to imagine standing in a London street between rows of tall, ornate Victorian houses made of water.*

When these elaborate structures collapsed over the decks, they sometimes buried the bow completely. At other times the ship heaved sideways with such force that she rolled close to

---

*Members of the expedition, including the many experienced seamen aboard the *Terra Nova*, referred to their experience south of New Zealand as "the gale." Sir Francis Beaufort's famous wind scale—devised around 1805 and first used officially in 1831 on the voyage of the *Beagle*, made famous by Charles Darwin— identified Force 9, Force 10, and Force 11 as "strong gale, whole gale, storm." In more modern versions of the scale, these are "strong gale, storm, violent storm." Waves in the region of thirty-five feet normally suggest wind speeds of 60 to 65 miles per hour (52 to 56 knots), consistent with Force 10 to 11. But the Southern Ocean is notorious for producing huge swells even in relatively mild winds, so it may have been blowing "only" Force 9. Whatever the actual wind speed, the wave conditions were at the absolute limit of the overloaded *Terra Nova*'s endurance.

her limit. She wrestled the force of the waves, but there were moments when all the fight seemed to go out of her. She relaxed as she heeled over, continuing to roll until standing on the railings made as much sense as standing on the deck. Then, for a few sickening moments, she would hang there, with the waters licking at the leeward edge of the main hatch, and despite all the activity on board, everyone seemed to stop breathing. Slowly, like a wounded animal summoning every last ounce of strength to cheat death for the sake of the helpless cubs clinging to her sides, she would pull herself upright again. To reduce the danger of rolling, Captain Scott gave the order to start dumping coal. Sacrifices to Neptune! We offered five tons or more to the sea god in return for our lives. We were travelling to a place where sources of heat are something one never wastes. In this storm, we had no choice.

Mighty Osman, who came back from the dead

My cabin, on the port side, was chaos. Nicknamed the Nursery, because it was home to some of the younger expedition members, it had been designed for four seamen, but on this expedition it was home to six scientists, their gear, a Broadwood Pianola, and a cabinet containing 250 rolls of music. The storm so strained the ship's deck that water poured in between the boards and cascaded off the top of the Pianola. Our clothes and books, neatly stowed in New Zealand, were either drenched in their places or floating about in the foot-deep swill on the floor.

I barely had time to notice this devastation when suddenly there was something worse to think about.

The *Terra Nova*'s boilers powered a mechanical pump. A wooden ship will always leak a little, especially when its timbers are stretched and stressed by a heavy sea. But the *Terra Nova* was leakier than most, even after its repairs in Lyttelton, and even in normal conditions we were forever taking turns at the hand pump just behind the mainmast, to help keep the water level down. With the storm and the clogging lumps of coal-and-oil, it was not enough. The water kept creeping upward. Finally it came within inches of the boiler plates. This threatened immediate catastrophe: at worst, a steam explosion that would rip the ship in two; at best, buckled metal and a permanently useless boiler. Captain Scott ordered fires drawn; our only source of power, except for the maddened wind, was shut down.

Stopped engines were two problems rolled into one. Without power, we could not steer well, so it was even harder than before to keep pointing into the waves. (In a storm, one must either face the waves or flee before them. As we had already found out, allowing them to approach from the side increased the threat of being rolled over.) But having no engine also meant that the mechanical bilge pump no longer worked. If we could not pump out more water than was coming in, we would never relight the boilers.

The *Terra Nova* was now at 52° South by 172° East, as near as we could tell. Our closest links to civilisation were little-used shipping lanes, mere goat tracks in the grey wilderness, and even these were hundreds or thousands of miles to the north. There was no help for us.

Our problem was easy to solve, in theory. Clean out the

pumps. Lower the water level. Light the boilers again. But we could get to the pumps only by opening the main hatch, and doing this in a Force 10 gale would have been suicide, as the hold would have flooded immediately. So Scott's second in command, Lieutenant Teddy Evans,* came up with a different plan.

"We'll have to cut through the bulkhead, sir."

A bulkhead is just a wall across the inside of a ship. Unfortunately, as Scott and Evans knew, this particular wall, separating the boiler from the pump well, was made of iron.

Working the hand pump: (facing camera from left) Bowers, A.C.G., Taylor, Wright

---

*Lieutenant Teddy Evans, who was part of the Polar Support Party, should not be confused with Petty Officer Edgar "Taff" Evans, who went to the Pole with Scott.

"How long?" Scott shouted the words, but they sounded like a hoarse whisper against the wind.

Evans shrugged. "Twelve hours, Captain." Then his reply was torn away by the wind, and it looked as if he was just soundlessly mouthing "If we're lucky."

In a crisis, there are moments that have the power to make men crack and fail, like overstressed timber. I remember sensing that this might have been such a moment. My own stomach sank, because I knew that there just were not twelve hours to spare. If the wind kept raging and the water kept coming in, twelve hours from now we would be shaking hands with our ancestors. How ridiculous it would be, after all the bold thinking, the big plans, the fund-raising and celebrating and trying on of fur mittens, to die beneath this loneliest of oceans without ever seeing the ice we had come to conquer!

Yet nobody cracked on the *Terra Nova* that day. Someone yelled "Right, boys, look sharp!" In an instant we were back at our places, either bailing like demons in the stoke-hold or hacking and hammering in the engine room, praying that three iron buckets would save us before one iron bulkhead became the death of us.

In the end, it took even longer than expected to get to the pump blockage and clear it. Teddy Evans's men started their work with the hammers and chisels around the time we should have been eating our Friday breakfast. It was ten o'clock that evening before Evans was able to crawl through a jagged opening, slither across a mound of coal, and dive under the flood to claw the fistfuls of muck from the pumps. We had already been working to save the ship, with no rest and one mug of cocoa each, for thirty hours. Evans stood in that freezing water, wrestling with the pump mechanism, for the rest of the night. There were many more hours of cold, drudgery, and danger before the water was low enough to start the boilers, and we were well into another day before the *Terra Nova* was truly dry again.

But Neptune had decided to spare us. Long before the bulkhead gave way, the wind eased, the sea slackened from terrifying to merely rough, and I began to feel confident once more that we would live to see Antarctica.

●—●—●

I will never forget that storm, in all its ferocity and horror. Funnily enough, though, my most vivid memory is of something even stronger than the storm, something that seemed to defy and contradict it.

In those days, I did not know Birdie Bowers well. I knew only that the quiet Scotsman was ugly, short, and outfitted with the muscles of an ox. And I was aware, also, of his reputation among the Naval officers as a superb navigator, the kind of man who can glimpse a single star through a rip in the clouds and know instantly what star it is, what time of day it is, and his ship's exact bearing. Yet it amazed me when, with the storm at the pinnacle of its fury and me unable to think of anything except what it would be like to drown, he waded past me in the rushing waters on the deck, loudly . . . *singing*.

Perhaps he saw my jaw drop. With the Southern Ocean clawing at his shins, he stopped, grabbed my shoulder, and

flashed me an enormous grin. His expression seemed to say, more clearly than any words, "Isn't it good to be alive? Isn't this fun? What a terrible pity to be anywhere else!" Then he moved away down the deck, singing even louder.

To be cheerful at such a time, in such a place! I wondered for a moment whether perhaps Birdie was mad. But Captain Scott, always good with words, had come up with precisely the right word for this man. *Undefeatable.* And I remembered something Bill had said, one sun-blasted afternoon early in the trip. We were somewhere off equatorial West Africa. Uncle Bill and I were examining an enormous jelly-fish that we had abducted from the ocean and placed in a large jar of water on the deck. I lay on my stomach, gazing in at the pulsing white apparition, while Bill sat cross-legged on the other side of the jar, sketching it.

Ugly, short, and undefeatable: Lieutenant Henry Robertson Bowers

"What do you make of Birdie?" I asked casually. I was only making conversation, and Bill could easily have said "Oh, he's a fine chap" and left it at that. Instead, he put down his pencil and hunched forward, fixing me with his bright eyes and thin, ironic smile over the top of the jar. After a long pause, very quietly and slowly, he said this:

"I am beginning to suspect that there is something very unusual about Lieutenant Bowers. He said the other day that he was afraid of spiders. I'm not sure I believe him. I don't think he knows what fear *is.*"

"Well," I replied rather foolishly, "that might prove useful. Where we're going."

Oxo in the Antarctic

A Photo from Capt. Scott

This is a reproduction of a photo just received from Captain Scott. Large supplies of Oxo were purchased by him to sustain the members of his Expedition.

* * *

It will be remembered that Oxo was also the stand-by of Sir Ernest Shackleton's Expedition a few years ago.

* * *

All who value stamina should follow the lead of those who have made diet a special study and drink Oxo. It is easily-assimilated nutriment and, unlike most other foods, none of the energy it creates is lost in the process of assimilation.

ELEVEN O'CLOCK OXO ON BOARD THE TERRA NOVA.
FROM A PHOTOGRAPH TAKEN IN THE ANTARCTIC RECEIVED FROM CAPT. SCOTT.

3

WHITE CHRISTMAS

SOUTHERN OCEAN, DECEMBER 1910
TO JANUARY 1911

AFTER THE STORM, we enjoyed several days in which the weather was merely horrible. The waves were smaller but steep and confused, bumping past one another like a crowd of self-important men in great-coats at a train station. The *Terra Nova* bucked and shook. No longer fearing for my life, I had to think about the motion and was even more violently sea-sick than during the gale. Birdie, by contrast, was not bothered by the waves at all and was busy showing off one of his other peculiar virtues, a superhuman indifference to the thermometer. It was much colder now. The rest of us had started resorting to woollen hats, thick leggings, and mittens, all crusty from the salt bath they had taken in the storm. Meanwhile, Birdie continued to stride about the deck in a cotton undershirt. Standing near the prow, casting an expert eye over the waters, he looked like a man anticipating landfall in Hawaii.

He even maintained, this close to the Antarctic Circle, a routine that everyone else had long since abandoned. Each morning, in warmer climes, we would strip naked, fill a bucket

This advertisement for one of the expedition's sponsors was closely based on a photograph—except for the sea in the background. It was flat calm and ice-free that day

from the little hand pump near the mainmast, and get a good wash. Now the pump was useless, feathered with ice like some tropical bird gone far off course, but Birdie still went to the same spot, at the same time. Using a rope, he would haul up a bucket of icy slush, dump it over his head, and flush bright red all over, like a cooked lobster. He seemed to find the experience refreshing.

We watched, smiled, and shook our heads. "Ordinary men are made from flesh and bone," Scott muttered. "Birdie, I am beginning to think, is made from some other, stronger material."

⬤━⬤━⬤

Thursday, 8 December, dawned hazy, but the sea was mercifully calm, and towards noon the sun broke through. A pleasant cruise at 64° South, and to add to the general feeling of picturesque tourism, a veritable fleet of blue whales steamed across our wake. Late in the afternoon someone spotted a snowy albatross. Uncle Bill was just starting to make a charcoal sketch of it on the only thing available, a scrap of sailcloth, when a shout from the lookout interrupted his artistic endeavours.

"Icebergs! Icebergs on the port bow!"

Admittedly, they were twenty miles away. To see them, we had to take turns scrambling up into the crow's nest.* But

---

*A precarious barrel with a trap-door in the bottom, the crow's nest was attached more than a hundred feet up the mainmast. Bill spent countless hours there and referred to it as his "private chapel."

there they were, out to the east: two magical silver fortresses standing guard over the blue silk plain of the ocean.

Most southern icebergs are not the tall towers one sees in illustrations. More commonly they are broad, flat tables of ice that have broken off from the ice shelves surrounding the southern continent. But this made them all the more exciting, somehow. They were floating emissaries, island fragments of Antarctica itself!

The excitement lasted all evening and was with us still the next morning, but then it gave way to a different emotion. As the chunks of ice multiplied in the water and the sea thickened to the consistency of soup, we grasped that our beautiful silver fortresses were a sign of something gone wrong. We had come south too soon, before the spring thaw.

In New Zealand, Captain Scott was all for an early departure, with good reason. "I want us to be in Antarctica," he said, "setting up camp and testing equipment, with every possible minute of the southern summer and southern light still available." It made good sense at the time, in the way of plans that are conceived over a calendar and a pot of tea in a warm conference room. We had a lot of work to do before the months of darkness closed in, and we wanted plenty of time for it. Nature had other plans. Before noon, still almost two degrees north of the Antarctic Circle, we ran up against the pack ice.

A band of sea ice forms on the Antarctic Ocean every winter. Depending on where you are, it can be fragile as paper or twenty feet thick. Wind and higher temperatures break it up in the spring. At this latitude, we expected to find ourselves in a

Three weeks without being sea-sick: the Terra Nova *imprisoned*

region of loose chunks and occasional bergs. Instead, farther north than any other ship before us, we had found an impenetrable barrier. The only good thing was that we did not know its extent. In 1901, the *Discovery* spent four days in the pack. In 1908, Shackleton's *Nimrod* traversed it in just two. But we had entered a region of ice that would turn out to be four hundred miles wide.* It would hold us in its grip, forcing us to use up yet more of our precious coal as we backed and pushed, trying to find a way forward, for three long weeks.

---

*Polar explorers usually give all distances in nautical, or "geographical," miles. This practice makes land journeys sound shorter than they are, since a march of 400 nautical miles is actually 460 of the more familiar statute, or "road," miles. A nautical mile is one minute (one-sixtieth of a degree) of latitude; one knot is one nautical mile per hour.

The expedition photographer Herbert "Ponko" Ponting cinematographing bumpy progress through the floes

I do not get sea-sick when more or less stationary, and I found other good things about an unplanned holiday in the southern pack. On some days, when we located leads, or cracks in the ice, and made a few bumpy miles of progress, we discovered that the *Terra Nova*, still overloaded but with her massive oak reinforcements, was much happier cracking ice than facing a storm. On bad days, we were stuck fast, but if we were lucky enough to have sunshine, the blue-tinged white of the ice, trapped between indigo water and a sky the colour of cornflowers, was a breathtaking sight. Then the "nights" eclipsed the days: around midnight, when the sun came down for its brief daily dip in the sea, the ice would shade to pink and purple while the whole sky shifted from palest blue to the yellowy green of an unripe lemon.

Another good thing about our imprisonment was that we and our canine companions had the freedom to get off the ship for exercise. There was time to stretch and run. When the dogs were satisfied and were lolling near the ship with their eyes closed and their tongues hanging, there was time to write our diaries, sketch the landscape, and watch for the plumes of passing whales.

Flocks of delicate fulmars and petrels would wheel above the ship, crying *why why why*. As well they might. The pack

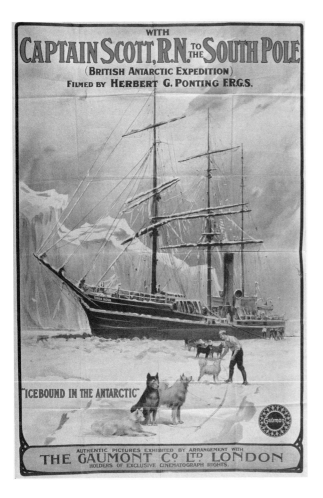

Audiences saw some of Ponting's film footage under this title as early as the end of 1911; it became the film 90° South in 1933

ice was also our first opportunity to greet the funny men of the Antarctic, the busy, curious little Adélie penguins, junior cousins to Bill's Emperors. Their wedge-shaped heads and bright eye rings made them look permanently surprised. Rushing the *Terra Nova* in crowds, they would show off their white shirt-fronts and squawk to one another as if competing to explain this unprecedented visit from a smoke-breathing whale. The penguins even approached the dogs, having no idea that they were risking a bloody death, so Titus and the Russian dog-handler, Dimitri Gerof, had to stand on the ice waving sticks to keep them away. The Adélies showed fear, diving off the floes and vanishing, only if they sensed the presence of the creature that takes the place of dogs in their world—the gruesome "sea leopard," a huge-jawed seal four times the weight of a man, with a murderous disposition and teeth like rows of sharpened chessmen.

Early in the morning of 10 December, after more than a week of slow, bumpy progress, we crossed the Antarctic Circle. The sun no longer set at all but merely knelt down to kiss the horizon before lazily rising again. The quality of the light did change over the course of twenty-four hours, but it never failed, and its endless energy was infectious. We felt so alert that each of us could do the work of three men and we scarcely bothered to sleep. It was wonderful: it gave me confidence that we had the strength Antarctica would demand of us. I was almost right.

I used every minute of the time in the ice, every ounce of that superabundant energy. Still conscious that I owed my berth on the *Terra Nova* to dumb luck, I volunteered for the hardest jobs, learned the rudiments of seamanship from Birdie, and begged for extra coaching in the fine art of travelling by ski from our Norwegian expert, Tryggve Gran. But my greatest satisfaction came from discovering something important at which I really did turn out to be useful. On the sunnier days, my glasses did not frost over. When they were freshly polished, I was a decent shot with a rifle and could bag a crabeater seal with little difficulty.

Those charming little Adélies were not among my targets, but only because I could catch them by lying down in the snow and waiting until their curiosity brought them waddling into my arms. On one occasion this lazy method of hunting for dinner did turn exciting: the dogs saw me with two struggling birds under my arms, and I had to sprint back to the ship fearing that at any moment I would have the bottom ripped out of my trousers.

⬤⬤⬤

Imagine me now, trying to focus on a book about navigation as I loll in the sunshine near the *Terra Nova*'s stern. Half a mile away, sitting on the ice with charcoal and an artist's easel, is Uncle Bill. He is creating a painstakingly accurate sketch of a sun-bathing Weddell seal, or perhaps a big, hatchet-headed bird, McCormick's skua, as it rests briefly from its life of thieving and savagery. It is impossible to paint out there on the ice, because the fingertips go numb and then the colours themselves freeze solid. So Bill's charcoal sketch will come back to the ship spidered with his own shorthand ("l pr bl fad to l pur" means "light Prussian blue fading to light purple"). Later, in the warmth of the cabin, he will transform his code into a painting.

Bill's paintings, dozens of them, were just a hobby: Doctor, Zoologist, and Chief of Scientific Staff were his official titles. Unlike me, he was a deeply religious man, but religious in a way that even a doubter could appreciate. Bill always had a certain look in his eye when he painted animals and scenery. For him, every seal and bird, every iceberg and streak of cloud, was a fragment of God.

As Chief of Scientific Staff, Uncle Bill was my "boss." Having judged that I would not disgrace the expedition by joining it, Scott decided to make things look better, or make me feel better, by crowning me with the glorious title Assistant Zoologist. Well, I swear to you, I knew far too little about zoology, but I could have turned all the continents inside out and not found a better man to assist. Bill was friendly, kind, and serene. He was also eager to teach me everything he knew, whether about medicine, the evolution of fish, or how to skin and mount a Sooty Albatross, to name just a few among a hundred skills and subjects. Unfortunately, this ambitious educational programme was like trying to stuff an elephant into a walnut shell. But he never lost his enthusiasm for the game.

Naturally, I thought well of him for all this. Later, I came to think well of him for other reasons, too: because, while leading Birdie and me on a journey to hell and back, a journey so ghastly that I doubt I have the language to describe it, he showed how a man can balance the virtues of the pagan hero with those of the Christian saint. On top of that, he was blessed with a virtue that heroes and saints invariably lack—a sense of humour.

Bill and Birdie, already fast friends, made an odd pair. Bill was an inch taller than me but weighed less and was ruggedly handsome. Birdie, the sailor, was almost six inches shorter than me but weighed more—all muscle, I should add—and had the vast hooked nose of a parrot, hence the nickname. Bill had a pale face and talked with a scientist's quiet intensity about books and ideas. Birdie's complexion was as red as his hair, and his words were few. The two of them seemed as different as the two halves of a comedy team, yet their friendship made sense. They shared . . . something. Some strength, some inner reserve of possibility, that I was only beginning to fathom.

Two hunters: Bill taking aim on deck, and his drawing of a sea leopard closing in on its next meal

By Christmas Day, four days after the start of the Antarctic summer, we were still stuck in the ice. Whenever I heard a grinding noise, I was unsure whether to think it was the ice against the *Terra Nova*'s bow or Captain Scott's teeth. ("This ship simply eats coal," I heard him mutter, exasperated at the waste.) But there was no better place for Yuletide celebration. We played football on an ice-floe in the endless light. When we had exhausted ourselves, we decorated the wardroom with our sledging flags and sang with more gusto than skill while someone played the banjo. Afterwards we consumed an unorthodox feast that started with salted almonds and tomato soup, went on to roast penguin breast as well as roast beef with Yorkshire pudding and asparagus, and ended with mince pies, plum pudding, and liqueurs. Soon after we finished eating, a picturesque snow began to fall.

The next few days were calm. Not a fact anyone thought to remark on, because it had been calm most of the time for weeks. But the leads were getting wider. Then, on the night of 29 December, the wind rose, and an hour or so before breakfast I noticed something odd. Subtle it was, about every nine or ten seconds, regular as the distant tolling of a bell. *Movement.*

When I came out on deck, I could see thin, dark leads opening all around us. We were bobbing, by just a few inches, on a long ocean swell. The ice was breaking up! A cheer rang through the ship as Captain Scott stood on the foredeck and fairly bellowed: "Fire her up, boys! We're getting out of here!" After sixteen hours of pushing and squeaking through icy rubble—exactly at the stroke of a bright, clear midnight—we surged forward into the open sea.

Our freedom came 250 miles beyond the Antarctic Circle, just past 71° South. By an odd coincidence, this was the latitude at which, in January 1774, the greatest explorer of them all first ran up against the pack. This point, so close to the goal, was where Captain James Cook, sailing the *Resolution*, was forced to turn back, giving up his search for the mysterious continent he believed was there but never saw.

Terra Australis Incognita, he called it. The Unknown Southern Land.

4

SEVENTY-SEVEN SOUTH

CAPE EVANS, JANUARY TO APRIL 1911

ON A NORMAL New Year's Eve, you would find me up late with all the other carousers, glass in hand and full of song. But I spent the final day of 1910 on deck, helping Birdie sort stores for ten straight hours in the wind and sun; I was too tired for the thought of celebration to cross my mind. After demolishing a large plate of seal stew, I shuffled back to the Nursery at 8.30 P.M. with my eyes half-closed. I slumped onto my bunk, delighting in the thought of a full night's sleep and fully expecting to wake up in 1911.

Instead, my first rude awakening occurred in the extreme rump of 1910. I had been in my bunk for only two hours when I was startled awake by a sound far more interesting than a chiming clock or a popping champagne cork. Someone was hissing in my ear: "Cherry! Cherry! You've got to wake up. Land!"

On deck, half-dressed and rubber-legged, I rubbed my glasses on a filthy shirt and joined the crowd at the rail. At first, even with the glasses in place, I couldn't see a thing.

Shore Party: (standing) Taylor, A.C.G., Day, Nelson, Teddy Evans, Oates, Atkinson, Scott, Wright, Keohane, Gran, Lashly, Hooper, Forde, Omelchenko, Gerof; (seated) Bowers, Meares, Debenham, Wilson, Simpson, Taff Evans, Crean (Ponting took the picture; Clissold was sick and is not present)

Then I made out a pale band in the sky just above the horizon.

"I can only see clouds," I muttered, wondering if I was really squinting at some newly discovered continent of grease on my lenses.

"Cherry, old man, those aren't clouds. Those are snowfields. That's Mount Sabine! The Admiralty Range!"

I was intensely happy at that moment. People talk about their dreams coming true. Now I knew what that meant. Antarctica! I stood there for three minutes, staring, slack-jawed with delight.

However, sleep is sleep. Leaving the chattering throng behind me, I drifted back to my bunk and got to enjoy once again the sensation of being enveloped by a warm blanket and the even softer weave of unconsciousness.

An hour later I was woken up again. It was midnight: some roistering fool was blowing the ship's whistle. A minute after that, the door burst open, and Griff Taylor stumbled in singing a sea-shanty. He was followed by Trigger Gran, who sat down at the Pianola (which happened to be next to my ear) and started to play. A third interloper thrust cocoa into my hand. I suspect that Gran was still playing the Pianola when I fell asleep for the third time.

●━●━●

The first morning of the new year drenched us in sunlight. At five o'clock, despite a steep swell, the whole ship's company turned out for an unscheduled session of loud, joyous hymn-

Cape Crozier and the Knoll in relatively warm weather

singing. Or hymn-shouting: the noise we made was barely musical, but it was a big, happy noise, even from the most bleary-eyed among us. Everyone was grinning.

We were still a hundred miles from land, and we fought our way south all day through a steep, unpleasant swell. But Monday, 2 January, was my birthday, and by way of a gift we caught a distant glimpse of the active volcano that James Clark Ross, who came this way in 1841, had named after his ship: Antarctica's great, steaming god, Erebus. Soon we were off the northeast corner of the island he named after himself—Ross Island. Above us loomed the extinct volcano Mount Terror, which he named after his other ship.

In front of us lay Cape Crozier, Scott's first choice for a landing, and the place where I would almost lose my life in a few months' time. The north coast of Ross Island is open to the sea, except for seasonal fringes of sea ice. But on the southern and eastern side, it is attached to the Antarctic continent by what Ross named "the Great Icy Barrier." This is not sea ice but rather a permanent ice shelf hundreds of feet thick and as large as France; next spring, the Polar Party would have to cross it on their way to the Polar Plateau. Since the ice shelf meets the sea at Cape Crozier, it seemed an ideal place to set up shop for the Southern winter, which would arrive in June.

Ideal, other things being equal. Unfortunately, there was a strong ocean swell. We launched the whaleboat and rowed off to explore, but there was nowhere to land. After we were nearly smashed to pieces by a big chunk of falling ice, Scott hurried us back to the safety of the ship. "We'll have to think again," he said.

If Scott was disappointed, Uncle Bill was even more so. This was where, on his earlier expedition to Antarctica, Bill had discovered the breeding ground of the Emperor penguin. He badly wanted to return, and landing there would have made his investigations simple. Instead he had to do his science the hard way.

Our second-best choice was McMurdo Sound, at the other end of the island, where the *Discovery* expedition had had its base. Lieutenant Evans turned the ship westward and cruised along the barren north coast, black and white and treeless.

On 4 January, we turned south into the Sound, passing the hut Shackleton had built in 1907 at Cape Royds. There was still open water ahead, and since every mile farther south was a mile less of dragging sledges, the *Terra Nova* sailed on. Finally, near a triangular spit of land that had been known to the 1903 expedition as the Skuary, the ice came together and made the way impassable. "Cape Evans!" Scott declared, renaming the featureless tongue of gravel after his second in command.

One had to wonder whether Scott really meant it as a compliment or not, and whether Evans took it for one: the two men were never the best of friends.*

This "landing place" was better than the forbidding cliffs we had passed earlier, better than the surf-pounded, boulder-littered beaches. But it was not land at all. Between *Terra Nova* and *terra firma* lay more than a mile of sea ice. Never mind: it would do. We began the work of unloading and hauling.

Although I was painfully aware that we had overloaded the ship, it was still astonishing to see her disgorge her contents onto the ice. There were seven Navy officers and twelve ordinary seamen in the Shore Party, plus ten members of the scientific team, two Russian animal handlers, seventeen surviving ponies, and thirty surviving dogs. We were planning to be here, an infinite distance from the nearest corner shop, for two years. Try to imagine the mountain of food, fuel, and equipment we needed—then treble your estimate.

The unpacking was hard labour, but after nearly wasting our lives in the gale and wasting three weeks in the ice, we had arrived at Cape Evans with immense optimism and energy. Now we could get down to the serious work of preparing for the expedition! The animals thought that flat ice and open

---

*Even Birdie—in the privacy of a letter to his mother—complained about Evans, calling him fawning and insincere. "I would almost rather see a man become truculent and quarrelsome," he wrote after seeing how Evans behaved around Scott, and added, "I think more highly than ever of our leader now." Scott's wife, Kathleen, also detested "that creature" Evans. But it may be that he was no worse than an insecure man among people who found it hard to imagine insecurity.

space were a grand excuse for a party: the dogs howled for joy; dogs and ponies alike rolled and kicked and pranced. Little did they know what terrible work lay ahead. Little did they guess the cruel fate that was our necessity: we planned to use them, and then eat them. Antarctica is not for the faint-hearted.

●━●━●

I had thought camp life would be the easy part. Hard work but safe. Warm, too: our newly-built hut had four inches of quilted seaweed in the walls. Instead, as if to remind us of our pathetic frailty and absolute loneliness, the first days and weeks in *Terra Australis* were punctuated by icy accidents and near-disasters.

First came the incident of Ponting and the killer whales.

Herbert "Ponko" Ponting was the expedition photographer. A fine one, too, though the fact that he insisted on being referred to as the Camera Artist may suggest to you that modesty was not his strong point.

Never mind. On 5 January, the day after our arrival, Ponko was already hard about his business. He had decided to investigate some icebergs that were frozen into the sea ice about a mile away

A train of two-legged pack animals unloading the Terra Nova *at Cape Evans*

More or less unpacked: 23 January 1911, Mount Erebus in the distance

and had just finished piling gear onto his personal "photography sledge." The rest of us were still busy unloading the *Terra Nova* when a group of eight killer whales came cruising along the ice-foot near the ship. Ponko was on the point of setting off for the icebergs when he spotted them. *Ah,* he must have thought, *killer whales hunting for seal, an excellent photographic opportunity.* At the same moment, Scott bellowed to him. "Ponting," he cried. "Ponko, old man! Killer whales! Get over here at the double and do your magic!"

Ponko grabbed some things off the sledge and came loping across the ice, his breath flowing behind him like a grey silk scarf. When he got a little closer, I could see that he had a wooden tripod jammed under one arm and was cradling his great boxy camera in both fur-mittened hands. He managed to get to the scene without a mishap, but by then the glistening beasts had disappeared. Undeterred, he took up his position a few feet from the edge, at a point near where two of the dogs were tethered.

It was a beautiful day: a sapphire sky wrapped like a jewel in the most diaphanous white tissue of cirrus. Besides, you just don't get thunder in Antarctica, so the first great boom, when it came, was puzzling. Even more puzzling was the fact that the dogs went into a snapping, leaping frenzy, and Ponko suddenly staggered backwards, doubled over as if he had been punched in the stomach by an unseen fist.

With the second boom, a crack appeared in the ice near Ponko's feet, but it was only after the third boom that we understood. This was the thunder of the Ross Sea. This was a group of killer whales with fresh dog on their menu. They had "disappeared" in order to prepare for a coordinated attack, and now they were using their huge, seven-ton bodies to "bomb" the underside of the ice. It was a yard thick: they shattered it like a china tea plate. As the pieces of ice began to drift apart, eight black heads loomed up above the surface. They did not look like the heads of living animals. They looked like the tar-black prows of pirate ships, sunk long ago but eerily returning to the world above the water, eager to claim new victims.

What happened next is hard to say except that everyone was shouting (or barking), and somehow our Camera Artist, leaping towards safety from ice fragment to ice fragment, narrowly escaped becoming a convenient source of protein. The dogs were terrified, but they were tethered just a few feet out of reach, and their attackers, after a long offended look, melted back into the water, leaving nothing behind but broken ice, a powerful scent of rotting fish, and, after the dogs calmed down, a deafening silence.

"My God," Scott muttered. "That was the nearest squeak I ever saw."*

We did not see the whales again that day, but we had learned a lesson. Killer whales are intelligent. They know what's happening up on the icy roof of their domain. Like wolves, they hunt in well-organised packs. This was not the last time they would offer us reason to fear them.

That evening in the hut, Victor Campbell, one of the *Terra Nova* officers, made a joke out of the incident. "It's a good thing you escaped," he said. "Imagine the humiliation, if a whale had eaten you because it thought you were a seal, and then spit you out again when it discovered you were only a photographer!"

Well, everyone except Ponko thought it was funny, anyway. But Ponting got the last laugh. After recovering his breath, he went on with that eventful morning's original plan and sledged out to the icebergs. Finding an ice-cave in one of the bergs, he went inside and took photographs of the *Terra Nova* from that vantage point. The "grotto," he called it. Remember: in 1911 photography was a recent invention. Those images of the *Terra Nova* displayed in an oval frame of ice were among the first to show people that this light box, this clever mechanical toy, could bring an entirely new kind of

---

*Later Ponko admitted, a bit sheepishly, that it was not the nearest squeak *he* ever saw: in fact, he said, "It was rather a case of déjà vu as far as I'm concerned." Four years earlier he had met an almost identical fate, in almost identical circumstances—except that the scene had been the heat of Calcutta in summer and the savage jaws had belonged to a maharaja's pet alligators.

beauty into the world. Ponko deserved "Camera Artist" after all.

◗◗◗

We had unloaded two of the three motorised sledges immediately. Putting them to work, we quickly fell in love with their strength. The smaller of the two could pull a ton of supplies at a time, and its stablemate's load was twice as much. But they were even more popular on the way back across the ice. After we had staggered along in their tracks, man-hauling our share to dry land on heavy wooden sledges, we would attach the empty sledges to the back of their motorised cousins and lie down, faces turned to the sun like so many daffodils, while we enjoyed a free ride back to the ship.

Perhaps that is why we were in too much of a hurry to unload the third sledge.

It was just three days after the Ponko incident. The weather had been surprisingly warm, the ice near the ship was getting slushy, and I was starting to feel nervous about leading the ponies across it. But we carried on with the work anyway, and on the morning of 8 January we managed to get the third sledge down onto the ice without trouble.

That day I was in a team of twenty men at one end of a rope. We were supposed to haul the vehicle onto safer ice before filling her tank and starting her engine. We did get her a few yards, but then she stuck in the slush. We heaved and nothing happened. We heaved again and there was a slight forward movement. Taking deep breaths and bending to our task, we heaved a third time.

Griff Taylor (in the white jacket) and Silas Wright in the ice grotto, with the Terra Nova *in the background. Ponko took this photograph on the afternoon of his near-miss with the killer whales. Minutes later, trying to climb the grotto berg, Silas slipped and nearly fell fifty feet into the water. As he sat congratulating himself on avoiding an icy swim, another killer whale surfaced at exactly the spot where he would have gone in*

Our labours were rewarded, at first, by nothing. No movement, no sound. Then we heard a cry as one of the men went in through the ice. Not a disaster, this: we had soon got used to falling through in weak spots, and the water was cold but not usually dangerous. But a second later there was a sickening two-toned crack, low and then high, like an oak tree splitting. "Drop the rope!" someone yelled. We stepped away from it and turned around just in time to see the big machine lurch downwards at one corner like an animal with a bad leg. Then, in the space of a second, it simply plunged, leaving our world forever and lashing out with its whiplike tail as it disappeared.

The man in the water was hauled out, but then another fell in amid the rubble of fractured ice. This time it was dangerous. Swift currents were flowing beneath the surface, and he was dragged out of sight under the ice. He would have drowned but for the fact that he managed to grasp a rope as he went under. Luckily there were friendly hands close by, so the damage was limited to a bad fright and a cold bath. But the water was sixty fathoms there. We had no hope of retrieving the sledge.

Scott, who examined the scene and declared it too dangerous to work, gave us the afternoon off. He blamed himself for the incident, which he considered a "disaster." But bad things are not always as bad as

Thin ice: the third motor sledge with only minutes to live

they appear. In reality, it was simply the beginning of a hard lesson. The other two sledges, which were supposed to take Scott hundreds of miles across the Polar wastes, proved almost useless, too, after their initial help with unloading the *Terra Nova*. Their oil froze. Their wooden patens slipped on the ice. Their pistons cracked. Nothing about their design was a match for the brutal cold.

The hut at Cape Evans, with icebergs in McMurdo Sound

●━●━●

Life seemed to calm down after the loss of the motor sledge. Our wooden base hut, prefabricated in New Zealand, was now home. We had warm shelter. Our cook, the sailor Clissold, produced a stream of mouth-watering meals, including exotic tinned treats like hare soup, vast rectangular pies filled with tinned gooseberries, or local specialities such as seal liver curry. We began to establish a routine of hunting, doing scientific experiments, and taking detailed weather recordings.

There was even time in the evenings for reading, talking, listening to Caruso on the gramophone, and dreaming of heroic conquest. We knew that only a handful of men would be included in the final Polar team that would leave late in the year, yet every one of us privately wondered, a dozen times a day, what it would be like to be chosen, to endure a thousand-mile march, and then to grin for the camera at Ninety South.

Amid such thoughts, two further near-disasters served to remind us that Antarctica is a terrible place in which to make small mistakes. The second of these killed three ponies, and very nearly killed Birdie Bowers, the Irish sailor Tom Crean, and me.

It was the end of the Depot Journey, a month-long sledging trip onto the Barrier to leave supplies of food and fuel at marked cairns for the Polar travellers. At One Ton Depot and Safety Camp, we left piles of meat, biscuits, and fuel, each marked by flags. They would lie there, conveniently frozen, for as long as needed.*

Returning from One Ton, on 21 February, we nearly lost an entire dog-team down a crevasse; these smooth-sided rifts in the ice, often concealed beneath fragile caps of snow, could be

---

*One Ton was so named because at least a ton of stores were left there. Safety Camp was the closest point to the Barrier Edge that was considered safe from the danger of breaking off into the sea. The "biscuits," a major part of the expedition diet, were a specially formulated ration, manufactured to Bill Wilson's specifications by the Huntley & Palmer Company. About 3 inches by 3½ inches, and ¼ inch thick, they were pale tan with a small "H&P" stamp on the front of each. Although they were usually eaten plain, there was a strong preference for frying them in penguin blubber.

a hundred feet deep. Only the immense strength of Osman, clawing at the edge, prevented the whole lot sliding in, and Scott still had to descend on the Alpine rope and rescue two of the dogs, which had slipped from their harnesses and fallen onto a snow bridge sixty-five feet down.

It took another week to reach the edge of the Barrier; when we did so, we saw at once that the sea ice was in poor shape. Thin and full of cracks, it would easily have been broken up by a seaward wind. But the only other way back to our camp would involve hauling overland across Cape Armitage. Scott gave the order to proceed over the ice around the Cape, "unless, of course," I heard him say casually to Uncle Bill, "things are really broken up further along."

Well. A small group under Bill left first, with most of the

Heading south to make supply depots: Bill and Birdie seated, Scott center, A.C.G. third from right

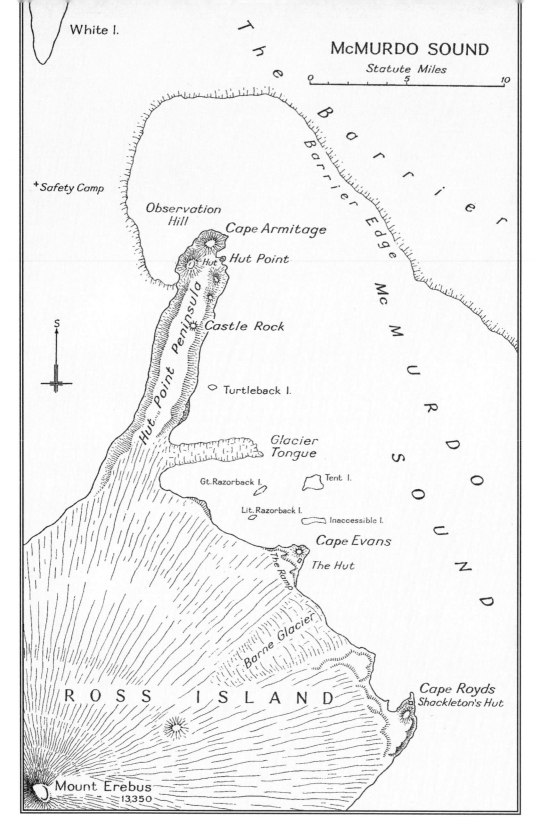

White I.

McMURDO SOUND

Statute Miles

The Barrier

Barrier Edge

McMURDO SOUND

+Safety Camp

Observation Hill

Cape Armitage

Hut · Hut Point

Hut Point Peninsula

Castle Rock

Turtleback I.

Glacier Tongue

Gt. Razorback I.

Tent I.

Lit. Razorback I.

Inaccessible I.

Cape Evans

The Hut

The Ramp

Barne Glacier

Cape Royds
Shackleton's Hut

R O S S   I S L A N D

Mount Erebus
13,350

dogs. My group (with Birdie and Crean) departed soon after with four ponies. It was night, and we were too far behind to see Bill's group in the poor light, but we followed their tracks. The ice didn't seem to get any worse, but to our surprise the dog tracks suddenly veered to the right. Bill had headed onto the Cape.

We wondered for a long time what to do, but Birdie was in charge, and instead of following Bill he followed orders. "Doesn't look all that bad," he said doubtfully, "and they'll have a hell of a time getting home overland." This last statement was true: Ross Island is criss-crossed with cliffs, rubble, and bad glacier ice. So on we went.

Poised over the ocean on this thin, cracked, soupy crust, we slogged on with our ponies and a big sledge for a few miles more. Then the ice really did get worse. We were not far from the safety of Hut Point, the old *Discovery* expedition hut, but our way was barred by open leads, and we wasted hours in detours and backtracking. Man and beast were equally exhausted—we had been on the move for about sixteen hours—but in the end it was necessary to retreat four miles south toward the Barrier; we assumed this would buy us enough safety to camp.

The tent went up at 2 P.M. Hurrying to cook for his hungry companions, Birdie then provided the only funny moment in a very bad day. He got his tins mixed up, and the fine, dark powder that he mixed with sugar and stirred into Tom Crean's mug was not cocoa. Tom drained off the whole mug before he realised anything was wrong. A nice steaming mug of hot Madras curry powder! Tom's expression suggested that it was the most invigorating cocoa he had ever tasted.

So much for the funny part. According to Birdie, who saved our lives by sleeping badly, both Tom and I were snoring like buffalo when some other noise caught his attention. It was 4.30 P.M. Thinking that one of the ponies had somehow got into our food, he stumbled outside in his socks to discover a terrifying scene.

All around us, the ice had broken up into chunks. The piece we were on was scarcely larger than our tent, and the smallest pieces were visibly rising and falling in the sea swell. My own pony, Guts, had disappeared: there was only an ugly black hole where, as far as we could tell, he had been tethered. The other ponies were on other floes, separated from us by the dark water; our sledge, with all our food and equipment, was teetering at the extreme edge, within moments of sliding in.

Birdie was magnificent then. After shaking us awake, he went to work like a demon, jumping from floe to floe in his sodden socks. He had rescued the sledge and the remaining ponies almost before we were standing upright. Then, after he had pulled his boots on, we turned our minds to solving a tough and dangerous puzzle.

I'm the sort of man who enjoys solving puzzles in a book. But a maze printed on a page has the decency to stay still, and it doesn't threaten to kill you if you get it wrong. We had to get to safety by moving to the next patch of ice we could reach, but the patches we could reach were not always the ones in the right direction, and they kept shifting. Sometimes a floe would move towards us, crash into the one we were standing on, and bounce hard enough to move out of reach again before we could get onto it. We made slow, frightening progress. Then our old friends the killer whales came to visit.

If you had asked me about killer whales before the incident with Ponko, I would have said that they were mildly interesting sea creatures. I would have agreed with you that they were dangerous, but not really felt the truth of it. After I had watched their coordinated efforts to eat our Camera Artist, they became for me the sort of animal that shows up in bad dreams.

There were about ten of them this time. Their fins were only yards away from us and reached six feet out of the water. The bolder animals raised their great heads to peer at us, actually propping their upper bodies on the ice, two flippers resting on the edge like the elbows of an unfriendly-looking man staring at you across a table. Or not, for the unfriendly-looking man may dislike you or want to cheat you, but even if he is a murderer he recognises, at some level, that you are a fellow

A killer whale looking for lunch

human being. The killer whales were different. Their small, unblinking eyes looked at me in a way that expressed the very different idea that I was a large chunk of meat.

Somehow we solved the maze, but not before two of our remaining three ponies, stiff from the cold, failed to make a jump between floes and were claimed by the freezing sea.

Thomas Clissold in the kitchen

This deadly game of musical ice lasted for hours, and I don't want to play another round so long as I live, thank you very much. Wet, hungry, and with finely shredded nerves, we got back to the safety of the Barrier and were able then to follow Uncle Bill's route to Hut Point.

Perhaps I should clarify: *my* nerves were shredded. Long afterwards, Tom remained stoically silent about the whole affair. Birdie finished our excursion by looking back the way we had come, laughing heartily, even though he had lost his favourite pony, and saying: "Well, that was interesting!"

●━●━●

And so the long winter began. For weeks after our little dance with the killer whales, we were stuck at Hut Point, waiting for that treacherous sea ice to harden. The ventilation was so bad that soot from burning seal blubber, which fuelled both our lamps and our stove, turned us black. It didn't matter much, though. One can go months in the Antarctic without washing or even changing one's clothes, because the bacteria that make a man stink have the sense not to make their home there.

Scott took some of the men back to Cape Evans on 13 April, over ice that was still thin and dodgy. Despite the primitive conditions at the *Discovery* hut, I was glad to be among those he asked to stay behind. We had to wait another week before the ice was thick enough to bear our return with the surviving ponies.

The day after our return to Winter Quarters, we took part in a bittersweet ceremony. Gathering on the shore in front of the Cape Evans hut, we greeted the sun for the last time before the long, long dark. Actually what we greeted was a half hour of pale golden glow in the northern sky, since the sun itself, barely struggling above the horizon, was hidden behind the Barne Glacier. But we made our respectful obeisance, standing there for the full half hour that it took for the light to grow and then fade again. Thus did the shortest day I had ever seen give way to the longest night.

All the big work of supplying the depots was done, and there was something profoundly comforting in knowing that, out there in the frozen wilderness, carefully prepared caches of food and fuel lay waiting for the weary sledge teams that would depend on them. Now we settled down to a season of reading, talking, and testing equipment. Our activities were punctuated by a strange musical tinkling from the darkroom: Ponko at work, developing his photographic plates and smashing the ones that did not meet his exacting technical and aesthetic standards.

There was also a schedule of lectures to help while away the time. Bill was excellent on Antarctic birds. Frank Debenham was far more interesting than we had any right to expect on rocks and minerals. We guessed that Titus, with his reputation as a quiet pessimist, would be dull as ditch water on the subject of "how to manage horses," but he was a fountain of jokes, some of the funniest ones quite unprintable. The most popular talk by far, however, was one that elicited no laughter, only wistful sighs: Ponting on his travels in Japan, complete with lantern slides of Mount Fuji, exotic temples, and geishas in a sunlit lotus garden.

Meanwhile, little bits of informal teaching were going on all the time, as the seaman Taff Evans taught one of the scientists the craft of boot-mending, Titus showed Taff how to fit a pony's harness correctly, or Ponko explained to Scott the mysteries of photographic technique. But for some reason the highlight of each day was Birdie and Bill's expedition, 250 feet up a rubble slope called the Ramp, to consult with "Bertram," the nearest of three weather stations. ("Archibald" and "Clarence" were out on the sea ice.) Having read and reread all our magazines to the point of disintegration, we even beguiled the hours by publishing one of our own. It was a continuation of the *South Polar Times*, which Shackleton had edited on the *Discovery* trip. As the only man in possession of a typewriter, I was privileged to follow in his editorial footsteps. Outside our little wooden world, our smudge of human warmth, it was permanent frozen night.

At work on the South Polar Times

I felt snug and well-rested; so did we all. But Bill's feet were starting to itch. A whispered conversation with Scott resulted in a curt, decisive nod of the head; Bill gathered Birdie and me to his side.

"What's on your mind, Uncle?" Birdie asked.

"Same thing that's been on my mind for the past eight years. Emperor penguins."

There was a faraway gleam in his eyes, the same gleam that I imagine lit up the eyes of Columbus, da Gama, and Magellan. He described in more detail the immense breeding colony he had investigated at Cape Crozier in 1903 and outlined his plan. Then, being a conscientious fellow who would not have wanted us to get into anything we did not fully understand, he finished by saying softly: "Now look. You must realise that what I am proposing is terribly, terribly dangerous. There is a good chance we will die. Nobody has attempted anything like this."

Birdie looked at me with an impish grin. It was the kind of grin you might find on the face of a small boy who has been offered a piece of chocolate cake along with the warning that it may be bad for his teeth.

"When can we start?" he said.

5

MAN-HAULING IN HELL

CAPE EVANS TO CAPE CROZIER,
JUNE TO JULY 1911

THE PLAN WAS simple. Mad, but simple.

Bill, Birdie, and I would go for a little walk. We would haul two enormous sledges behind us on this walk and they would be piled high with food, fuel, sleeping bags, and scientific equipment to the tune of more than 250 pounds per man. Dragging this burden, we would head due south to Hut Point, fifteen miles away across the sea ice, and then we would turn east and climb onto the permanent ice of the Barrier. All familiar territory, so far. But then we would continue northeast, for another fifty miles, right along the southern coast of Ross Island. Our destination was the same impossibly forlorn headland, at the intersection of Barrier and sea, where we had tried to land in January, Cape Crozier. At this spot, notoriously stormy even by Antarctic standards, we would claim our glorious prize. The unhatched eggs of an Emperor.

"As I told you, Cherry, I was at Cape Crozier during the *Discovery* expedition. Sledged there twice in the spring of 1903. Charming weather even then: gales strong enough to

"The weirdest bird's nesting expedition that has ever been or ever will be." Pitch darkness at eleven in the morning, Cape Evans, 27 June 1911

blow your boots off, and when the wind died it would go down to minus fifty-something. But at least we got ten hours of light every day. There's a shelf of sea ice, under the cliffs near where we tried to land the *Terra Nova*. An immense rookery. Very noisy, with an appalling smell even in the cold, and absolutely fascinating."

So fascinating, truth be told, that it was the reason Bill had agreed to come south with Scott a second time, despite the protests of his wife, Oriana. The Emperors, Bill believed, were a sort of biological master key.

"Tell me about this German chap," said Birdie.

"Haeckel, Ernst Haeckel. The best German biologist there is, and he has developed a very interesting spin on Darwin's ideas. The theory of natural selection solves the puzzle of how each kind of animal fits its place in nature so well. But it can't tell us exactly what happened along the way. Haeckel's idea is that you can read the history of how a species evolved by looking at how one of its *embryos* develops. Ever looked closely at a human embryo in its first month or so? It's amazing: you can see the gill slits on the neck. According to Haeckel, that's because we evolved from fish. In a nutshell, his theory is that the stages of an individual's early development repeat or mimic the evolution of its kind."

"Why does that matter?" I asked.

"It's like this, Cherry old boy. My observations suggest that the Emperor is the most primitive of all birds."

"You mean it belches after dinner?" Birdie interjected.

"Probably does. Probably does. But what I mean by *primitive* is simply that it looks like the creatures it evolved from.

Sharks are 'primitive,' because they look like their ancestors, which is just to say that their ancestors hit on a good design and stuck with it. We are not 'primitive,' because we became upright and hairless much more recently. Now, if Emperor penguins are primitive in that sense, and Herr Haeckel doesn't have his headpiece screwed on sideways, Emperor embryos will tell us the whole story of how birds evolved. I think birds evolved directly from dinosaurs. And I'm willing to bet you a large plate of roast beef and Yorkshire pudding that your young Emperor embryo, unlike its dear Mama and Papa, has both scales and teeth."

Ernst Haeckel and friends

"That's a bit rum," Birdie observed sagely. "Birds aren't supposed to have scales *or* teeth."

"Precisely. And if the Emperor embryos do, that'll prove they evolved from creatures that did!"

Trying to keep up with all this but feeling a bit foggy about the whole business, I asked Bill why he had not collected any of these toothy specimens on the *Discovery* expedition.

"Very simple, Cherry. There weren't any. What we found at Cape Crozier in September oh-three were thousands of adults and hundreds of small chicks. When we went back in

October, there were hundreds of adults and thousands of large chicks. Plus, in both cases, some abandoned eggs, solid as rocks, and dead chicks, which we collected by the armload. But all the live chicks were a couple of months old, at least. Which means . . ."

He trailed off, eyes bright, encouraging me to use my brain and fill in the blank.

"Live chicks in September. Right you are. So the eggs hatched in, er, August. And they started incubating in . . . July? June?"

"You've got the idea. The Emperors incubate their chicks, out there on the sea ice in the screaming winds of Cape Crozier, in the middle of the Antarctic bloody winter!"

Birdie grunted and scratched his ear. "Inconsiderate little blighters."

❧❧❧

Scott did not want us to go, of course: he knew how risky it was. He did not want us to go even though he had half-promised this trip to Bill before we left England. Now, faced with the realities, he worried that he would lose good men. Bill knew Scott, though, and he played the trump card. "Listen to me, Con. [Robert Falcon Scott. Only his wife and his closest friends called him Con.] This is the single biggest chance for the expedition to take part in a scientific breakthrough. Is this not what we came for?"

Bill laughed about the conversation, afterwards. He said he felt like a schoolboy, asking a favour of the headmaster.

They had walked up the slope behind the hut together. Bill had talked and talked, trying to be persuasive, then sensed that it was time to shut up. Scott had said nothing for a long time, looked at Bill as if about to speak, looked away again over the Sound. Finally, he turned to Bill one more time and jabbed him in the chest with the stem of his pipe. He had just four short words of advice concerning Birdie and me: "Bring them back alive."

●━●━●

In the Southern Hemisphere, Midwinter Day fell on 22 June. The darkest of the dark, but it was a beautiful night, exceptionally clear. When I went out with Gran to check on weather station Archibald, we found the stars so bright that they lit up the whole side of Erebus.

By Antarctic custom, Midwinter Day is a kind of unofficial Christmas, a celebration of the fact that the sun, hidden beneath the northern horizon, is beginning its slow return. Squeezed around the long wardroom table that evening, we sang, wore silly paper hats, and ate far too much. The menu, designed by Uncle Bill, advertised a nostalgic feast of English treats, though Clissold had tipped his hat to Antarctica by including seal soup. One of the courses, snapdragon, was more of a game than a food; it involved brandy-soaked raisins that were set alight and had to be taken from the bowl with one's bare fingers.

Afterwards, over a motley collection of liqueurs, I presented Captain Scott with our first edition of the *South Polar*

Food and Equipment for Cape Crozier

Birdie was master of stores for the whole expedition, as well as for the Cape Crozier journey; somehow he kept in his mind a continuously updated list of what one might find in a thousand packing cases, tins, and bags strewn across a dozen locations. He also turned himself into something of an expert on the history and development of sledging rations, gave two excellent lectures on the subject, and worked out exactly what we would eat on our egg hunt.

Because intense cold makes camp chores so difficult, we wanted to simplify everything, including our food. For Cape Crozier, therefore, we took only pemmican, biscuit and butter (essential for the body), and tea (surprisingly essential for the mind). Sugar would have been good for both, and we regretted not taking it. Pemmican, supplied in tins for the expedition by J. D. Beauvais of Copenhagen, was a major food source on all sledging trips. Made from dried meat and animal fat mixed with dried fruit and cereal, pemmican has a very high calorie content, tastes good, and keeps indefinitely.

On Scott's instruction, we started with three slightly different daily rations, but these we adjusted during the journey until everyone was eating 12 ounces of pemmican, 16 of biscuit, and 4 of butter. It is interesting that, although all three of us felt insatiably hungry or even starved, none lost a significant amount of weight. As a result, the Summit Ration for the Polar Party was based on this amount, but it was almost certainly not enough, not taking into account the extra stress of high altitude.

Birdie wrote up a manifest for Cape Crozier:

Stores	Weight in pounds
"Antarctic" biscuit	135
3 cases for biscuits	12
Pemmican	110
Butter	21
Salt	3
Tea	4
Oil	60
Spare parts for cooker, matches	2
Toilet paper	2
Candles	8
Packing	5
Spirit (for lighting stove)	8
Total Stores	**370**

Equipment	Weight in pounds
2 Nine-foot sledges	82
1 Cooker complete	13
2 Primus stoves filled with oil	8
1 Tent	35
1 Shovel	3.5
3 Reindeer sleeping bags	36
3 Eider-down sleeping-bag liners	12

1 Alpine rope	5
Repair materials and tools	5
3 Personal bags—spare clothing etc.	45
Lamp box, knives, and sharpening steel	21
Medical and scientific box	40
2 Ice axes	6
3 Man harnesses	3
3 Portaging harnesses	3
Cloth to make roof and door for igloo	24
Instrument box	7
3 Pairs ski and sticks	33

(At the last minute, the decision was made to leave the ski behind, on the grounds that they would add weight without providing any advantage.)

1 Pickaxe	11
3 Pairs crampons	6.5
2 Bamboos (for measuring tide at Cape Crozier)	4
1 Plank for door of igloo	2
1 Bag sennegrass (dried grass for boot insulation)	1
Bamboo and knife for cutting snow blocks to make igloo	8
Packing	8
Total Equipment	422
Total Stores and Equipment	**792**

Times, which we had typed up and bound in sealskin. He read from it, to everyone's amusement; since I had asked that all contributions be anonymous, the game was to guess who had written what. There were speeches, some of them a trifle slurred, but Birdie said that he could think of no words worth adding, and shuffled off muttering that he would rather show us something. A minute or two later, he emerged carrying a

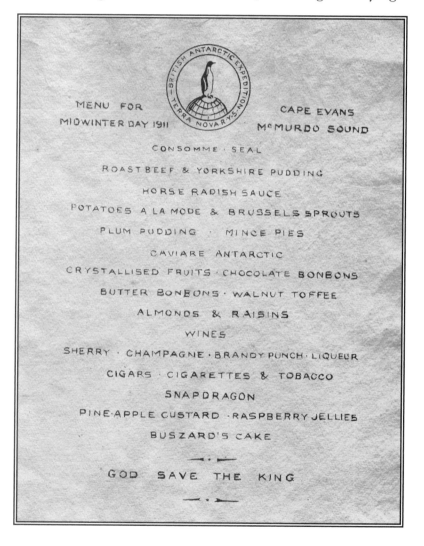

Bill's menu for the June celebration

"Christmas tree" he had made from pieces of bamboo, a ski stick, flags, and skua feathers. It was lit with candles and decorated with pieces of crystallised fruit and little presents that he doled out solemnly to each diner in turn. Titus, who received a child's pop-gun, spent the rest of the evening saying to people, "I say, would you mind awfully if I were to shoot you?" Nobody did mind. Griff Taylor even obliged him by groaning theatrically, clutching his chest, and falling backwards off his chair.

☙❧

Five days later, at eleven in the morning, Bill, Birdie, and I were all mittened up and ready to go. We posed with our sledges, and for half a second, as if in mockery of what we were about to experience, Ponko's magnesium flash turned the whole area at the back of the hut into a blinding tropical oasis.

I was still blinking away the retinal spots as we pulled out. When I tried to imagine a print of the photograph Ponko had just taken, it crossed my mind that a copy might go back to my family, sit in a nice silver frame above the fireplace for decades, and become a conversation piece for visitors. "Yes! That's the famous picture of dear old Cherry. Poor boy! So young to go out and die in a blizzard. But there he is, setting off on Bill Wilson's winter sledging lark. Still out there somewhere, down a crevasse probably. Nobody ever heard of them again; such a pity." I tried to soothe my nerves with the thought that at least I would be young all those years, as my family and friends withered into age beneath my gaze.

We had a good first day. The sea ice, rutted with small sastrugi,* gave us a poor surface to get started on, but it was an easy southerly course, due south through the little Dellbridge Islands (Inaccessible Island et al.), which poke out of the ice a couple of miles off the Cape to remind the passing traveller that he is walking on the thin skin of a frozen sea. We had company, too, those first few miles, because five of our colleagues, including Tryggve Gran and Dr. Taylor, decided to help us along. After a stop at Little Razorback Island, Taylor sent us off into the unknown with a custom-made toast for me, Birdie, and Bill: "Three cheers for the Cheery Winter Night, the Short Winter Night, and the Long Winter Night!"

That afternoon we passed Glacier Tongue, the big flow of ice down to the sea off the southwestern flank of Mount Erebus. When Bill called a halt, we did not even need to look at our sledge meter, a primitive wheeled device for judging distances, to know that we had done more than ten miles, almost a fifth of the distance to Cape Crozier. It was going to be so easy!

The one truly difficult part of that first day, a harbinger of worse to come, was making camp. We had already refined this simple routine on the Depot Journey and other excursions, so that we had it down like moves in a ballet. Drop the harnesses. Step up to the first sledge. Grasp the groundsheet and pull it out. Put the sleeping bags on top so the groundsheet can't blow away. Fix the poles. Everyone worked together, knowing exactly what to do next. The cook went in first, to light the

---

*A Russian word for irregular ridges in the ice, formed by the wind.

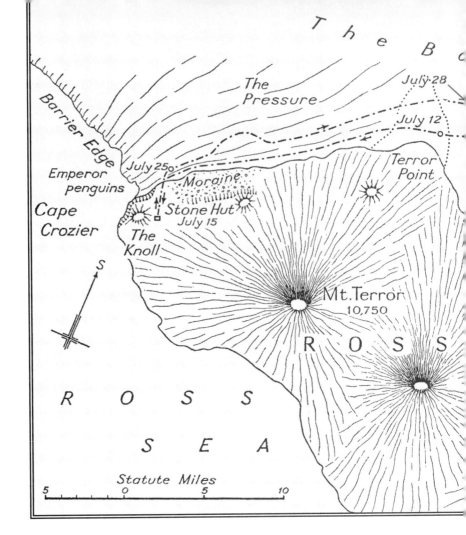

stove, while the other two piled snow against the tent sides and tied everything down. With military precision, we would ensure that there was a warm tent to enjoy just twenty minutes after stopping, though getting dinner cooked often took an hour.

That was in daylight.

Now we had darkness, and the darkness on that first evening was absolute. Bill had chosen our schedule so that we would get moonlight as we approached Cape Crozier and set up camp. There was none now, and despite a clear sky I could

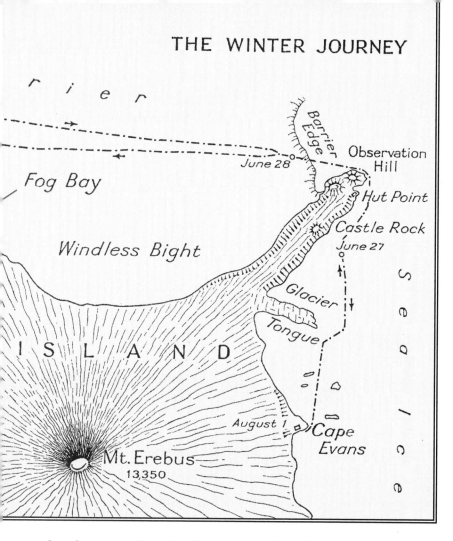

THE WINTER JOURNEY

r i e r

Fog Bay

Windless Bight

Barrier Edge

June 28

Observation Hill

Hut Point

Castle Rock

June 27

Glacier

Tongue

I S L A N D

S e a

August 1

Cape Evans

Mt. Erebus
13,350

barely see the hand in front of my face. Stumbling about like clowns in a hayloft, we found that five-minute jobs were consuming half an hour. By the time we all got into the tent, we were exhausted and dangerously cold.

Ah well, never mind. Our tent was a new double-walled model, constructed for us by Taff Evans after a design Scott had found in a book by the Norwegian explorer Otto Sverdrup. When it and the hot food had warmed us, my worries melted away. I felt strong, ready for anything. If this was a mad adventure, I was confident that I had chosen to pursue it with

Dinner and then sleep—if you can get warm enough (Bill's sketch)

two of the most dauntless madmen alive. About that much, at least, I was not mistaken.

◗◗◗

On the second day we stopped for lunch at Hut Point, then passed the southern tip of Cape Armitage and turned east. The hidden sun was still casting an hour or two of faint grey day around noon. Ahead of us, like a line of white cliffs, we could clearly see the Barrier.

In some places the Barrier is 200 feet high. At the western end of Ross Island, fortunately for us, it was barely twelve feet, and we had no trouble finding a place where the drifting snow offered a slope to ascend instead of a vertical face. On that slope we encountered a phenomenon that knocked the breath out of us, even though we expected it.

Everywhere, even in the Antarctic, the sea is like a blanket thrown around the shoulders of the land, moderating the coastal temperatures. As a rule, temperatures become more extreme the farther one gets from the sea: air on the Barrier is typically twenty degrees colder than it is on the sea ice. Because cold air is also denser than warm air, it wants to sink. Halfway up our little snow chute, a strong, frigid wind hit us. It was all that cold, heavy Barrier air, rushing down off the edge onto the sea ice like an invisible waterfall.

I was near the top of the slope, pulling on a sledge rope

while Birdie shoved from below. As I leaned back to take the strain, the rope began to slip through my clumsy fur-mittened fingers. Arctic mittens are thick for good reason, but it isn't easy to work a rope when each hand is encased in a puppet the size of an overfed house cat. I thought that a few seconds without them would not matter, so I cast their protection aside in favour of a better grip. This was a mistake.

It was Birdie's job to compile detailed meteorological records in the tiny preprinted columns of a special notebook. He had measured the air temperature on the sea ice after lunch as –26° Fahrenheit, in still air. On the lip of the Barrier it was –47°F, with a wind factor that made the effective temperature much lower still. My thin undergloves were not nearly enough protection.

Frostbite sounds painful, but this is misleading. If your fingers feel cold, they *feel*. Frostbite is what happens when your flesh actually freezes solid. All sensation disappears and, if the bite is bad enough, never comes back: your fingers drop from your hands like rotted twigs from the end of a winter branch.

Atch Atkinson demonstrates the "sausage effect" for Ponting after his run-in with a blizzard

I was luckier than that. Half an hour later, when we camped for the night, my fingers had not dropped off. No! They had blistered and started to swell. They throbbed all night, as they might have done if I had slammed them in a closing door. By morning they had acquired both the fatness and the shiny, sleek, over-stuffed look of pork sausages. What's

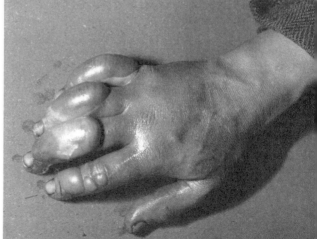

more, instead of having the decency to feel cold, or numb, they felt as if they were being grilled for breakfast over an open fire.

Funny place, the Antarctic. You sit there in your tent, trying not to think about the fact that the air outside is lethally cold. You munch your food silently, contemplating the day ahead. As you do this, you look at your hideous damaged hands and find yourself grateful that, despite your stupidity with the mittens, you still have fingers capable of causing you intense pain.

●●●

We were entering an area that would come to be marked, on maps not yet drawn, as Windless Bight. Looking at the shape of the land, one might suppose that the explanation is obvious. Here is a place, you might imagine in your ignorance, that is protected from northerly winds by Ross Island. How nice!

The truth is stranger and less pleasant. The prevailing winds here roar out of the south, down from the Polar Plateau and out across the Barrier. They aim due north, straight at Windless Bight and Ross Island behind it. But the ends of the island, at Capes Armitage and Crozier, are where that wind funnels downwards off the Barrier to the sea. So there is a "dead space" where the two winds divide, east and west.

As the name implies, Windless Bight is a place of almost continuous calm. Who could have guessed that hell has no flames?

Wind that stays cold as it moves can have a painful, dangerous bite, as my fingers had learned. But Seaman Lashly, recalling his days on the *Discovery* expedition, had warned us to expect worse of still air. "Wind out there on the Barrier warms you," he had said. "Stirs things up, I suppose." He supposed right. According to our weather man, "Sunny Jim" Simpson, wind mixes the cold surface layers with warmer ones higher up. Still air means that the layer near the ground, the layer in which you are endlessly trudging, just gets colder and colder and colder as the earth's warmth radiates away into space.

The worst effect of the extreme cold was the friction. At moderate temperatures—*moderate* being a relative term in these latitudes: I mean –20°F—the weight of the sledge runners melts a thin film of ice and the water "oils" them as they move. When it gets colder than this, the snow cannot melt and behaves instead like fine sand. That very first day on the Barrier, I found myself sneaking a look at the sledges, to see if the runners had fallen off. They became so hard to pull that they no longer felt like objects designed to glide. They acquired instead the feel of tree trunks, or rocks, or giant corpses. On the third night, the temperature plunged below –70°F. The next day, Friday, 30 June, the surface was so terrible that pulling both sledges at once was impossible: we simply could not move them. We had to start relaying, which is to say that we pulled one sledge for a mile and then went back for its twin.

Somehow it would have been bearable if switching to one sledge had made the hauling seem easy for a change. Instead, in that degree of cold, dragging even one sledge was an immense, gruelling labour. Worst of all, it ended with the depressing business of retracing our tracks, tense with the fear of losing our way, so that we could heave and cajole its companion over the same weary distance. At the end of that day, the results were dreadful. Eight hours of exhausting work. Seven and a half miles of travel. Two and a half miles of actual progress.

For hours at a time, during that terrible week we spent in Windless Bight, the air was so still that Bill was able to lead us with a naked candle, using one of several candle holders that he had fashioned out of pieces of biscuit tin. The flame stayed motionless, as if it, too, were made of wax. Meanwhile the daytime highs crashed to –55°F or below. At night, it was colder still. Bill got a frost-bitten heel, and I, still nursing painful fingers, could no longer feel either of my big toes.

In my mind I practised saying, "Doesn't look as if we'll be able to pull this off," and I imagined Bill replying, "You're right, Cherry. We had better turn back. Maybe we'll try again next year." But I kept quiet, and we kept moving. Imagine us: three hunched figures in the middle of the night, wrapped from head to toe like desert nomads, pulling across a white Sahara an impossible burden that might appear, in the candlelight, to be two dead camels.

❧❧❧

The cold bit into us like a thousand sharp teeth the instant we stopped moving. Paradoxically, though, the hard business of sledge-hauling made us hot and thirsty. "I want a pint of cold lime juice," Birdie said at one point, though it was minus God-knows-what and the drink he was dreaming of would have turned into a solid block on its way to his lips. As we puffed and sweated, each of us gave off just as many gallons of water vapour as any long-distance athlete. Yet the cold air of the Barrier is drier than any desert. It was in our finnesko that this difference first gave us trouble.

Finnesko are Norwegian boots made completely of reindeer fur. The fur goes on the outside, and they are cut big enough so that one can wear three or four pairs of socks inside. There is also sennegrass, a fine dried sedge that insulates and absorbs moisture, to stuff them with. Finnesko were invented, and ours were made, by the Lapps of northern Norway, who herd reindeer for a living. The Lapps know everything there is to know about warm boots. But we differed from the herders: we had no fires on which to dry our finnesko, and at the end of the day they were as damp as pairs of well-exercised spaniels. It was a great relief to peel them off. But removing one's feet from them allowed the frigid air to rush in, like a witch's curse, turning these soft, pliable, comfortable things to stone.

Finnesko. Immensely comfortable if warm and dry, "excruciating agony" otherwise

Because of this, the critical task, as soon as one got into the tent, was to take the boots off and arrange them in such a shape that there was some chance, the next morning, of getting them back on. Unfortunately, the only way for us to defrost these stone boots was by using our own feet. Scott once described putting on frozen

finnesko as "excruciating agony." He was not exaggerating. While eating breakfast, we would push our defenceless feet into these blocks for a few minutes and wiggle our toes, waiting until the risk of frostbite became too great. Then, with the sensation in our feet almost gone, we would remove them, rub like mad until the circulation returned, and repeat the process. Sometimes we would go through this cycle of self-torture four or five times. As a result, just getting into our boots in the morning—nothing else, just that—could take forty minutes to an hour.

Our sleeping bags were made of the same reindeer fur as the mittens, twelve pounds of it for each bag. They were still dry, more or less, but mine was too big and even then was barely keeping me warm. As the temperatures dropped, sleeping became worse than hauling, so that the mornings, despite the frozen finnesko, were a relief. Yet breaking camp was more of an ordeal as each day passed.

Straps, cords, and strings had to be tied and untied with our mittens on, but they were transformed by the cold into brittle wire. Eventually, even our clothes froze solid. Our best sledging position was hunched forward, back straight, head down. Alas, my first instinct when I emerged from the tent in the morning was always to stretch to my full height and take a nice long look at the sky. One such stretch was enough to teach me my lesson in those temperatures. In fifteen seconds flat, the moisture in the cloth froze my jacket and collar to the consistency of wood. I was stuck: using all my strength, I simply could not bend my neck into the right position. For four hours that morning, I pulled with my head up and my neck aching. Only when we stopped for lunch did Bill and Birdie, tutting and laughing at the same time, manage to hammer me into a better shape. After that, we learned to start the day by posing for a few seconds in the correct pulling position.

●●●

Amid all this difficulty, there were good moments. In the evening of Sunday, 2 July, about halfway across Windless Bight, Birdie suddenly cried, "Get your goggles on, Cherry! Look at that."

I kept my "goggles" wrapped in cloth, in an old pemmican tin on one of the sledges. Eyeglasses in Antarctica were nearly useless, because the moisture from my skin and my breath caused them to fog and then ice over almost the instant I put them on. I took them out only when there was something special to look at.

Behind us, after the usual rummaging and scraping, I discovered the source of Birdie's enthusiasm. The quarter moon, whose illuminations we had been so much anticipating, was rising directly out of the crater of Mount Erebus. Wreathed in volcanic steam, it gave the illusion of an unearthly, silvery eruption.

"Beautiful!" I breathed, instantly destroying the view with a rime of fine white crystals. Oh well. At least I had seen it. Back went my "goggles" into their tin.

A couple of hours later we stopped to camp. My frostbitten fingers were so painful that I was scarcely able to help. While Birdie cooked dinner, I sat there staring at my hands.

Then I found that it was too painful to hold my mug. Bill got out the housewife* and produced a large needle. At his urging, in an agony of exquisite relief, I popped the blisters one by one.

━●━●━●━

The next day was another slow, brutal slog in the minus fifties, and I was beginning to think that I could bear the cold and dark no longer. Yet even a day like this could surprise us with its grace and favour. Towards evening, in a moment of pure light-heartedness, Bill and Birdie flung themselves onto their backs in the snow. They wanted a better look at what Bill called "the most spectacular aurora australis I have ever seen":

"It's incredible, Cherry!"

"I wish you could see it!"

Ever the optimist, I once again dug out my spectacles; the lenses iced over before I could even get them settled on my nose. I could only see enough to know that I was missing something astonishing. I saw a few fragments of the *northern* lights once, in Scotland, but they were mere glimmers, like distant, hairy lightning. Now my entire field of vision was awash with shifting luminescence.

"The sky is on fire! It's breathtaking, Cherry."

And again: "I do wish you could see it!"

---

*Pronounced "hussif": a rolled canvas bag containing needles, buttons, thread, and other mending supplies.

Scraping and squinting one more time, I did see, just for a second, something unforgettable. Scott had described them as fiery writing sent down to us by the inhabitants of Mars; to me they simply looked like great rustling curtains—green velvet, gold brocade, and yellow silk—being drawn back and forth across the window of the night by an invisible hand.

⚫⚫⚫

When we awoke on 4 July, we were astonished to find that a light breeze was blowing and the temperature had climbed to –27°F. We were still in the supposedly "windless" area and could only imagine that we were feeling the gentle edge of a blizzard howling at the Cape.* Everything inside the tent became soaked, the surface conditions impossible. We were forced to stay in the tent and found ourselves so warm, relatively speaking, that we actually slept! In ordinary life, I could not have derived such pleasure from a month in Tahiti.

Of course, you pay for your pleasures. Next day the wind died and the temperatures crashed again. Every pliable object turned to armour-plate, and the new snow made for some of the worst pulling we had experienced. We could not even communicate without standing absolutely still, because our frozen clothes crackled loudly at the slightest movement. As if

---

*A ferocious storm *was* blowing, at Cape Evans, too, with winds over 50 miles per hour. Atch Atkinson went out that afternoon to take readings at Archibald and lost his way on the sea ice. He came within an ace of dying: he was found, severely frost-bitten, only after a six-hour search. The photograph of his hand, on page 87, was taken the following day.

that was not enough, the wind rose again in the afternoon, without any corresponding warmth this time. I marched with a solid plate of ice over the front of my Balaclava; it was a blessing, actually, because it functioned as a kind of igloo for my mouth and prevented my lips from freezing. We slaved until we thought our hearts would burst. My back and chest sweated profusely, but every other part of me was painfully cold. At the end of the day, unable to tell whether we were shaking more from cold or from exhaustion, we found that eight hours' labour had been rewarded with a new record of inefficiency. Our "distance made good"—actual progress across the map—was one and a half miles.

That night, as Bill prepared dinner, Birdie recorded a temperature of -75°F. The following morning—Thursday, 6 July, a date seared into my memory forever—it took nearly five hours for us to break camp and get under way. Why so very long? Had we gone soft, or become stupid with sleep deprivation? Not really. After a short march and a late lunch, Birdie took the thermometer readings as usual. But he did it twice, using two different thermometers, because he wanted to be sure that his eyes were not playing tricks on him. The news report from the little glass tube was stark, mad, appalling. In the middle of that day, when the date and time might lead you to visions of three men enjoying a picnic out of a wicker hamper under a bloom-laden chestnut tree, the temperature had dropped to the staggering figure of -77½°F. Bill, cheerful as usual but not having quite the intended effect, said brightly: "Fascinating! These must be some of the lowest temperatures human beings have ever experienced!"

As a matter of fact they were.* And they made the sledging surface so bad that even relaying became almost impossible. On that day and for several more, we pushed ourselves to the absolute physical limit of exertion, with abysmal results.

I truly believe that two more days of those temperatures would have killed us. But Mount Erebus's extinct twin, Mount Terror, was looming to our left in the moonlight, and then great scarves of fog wreathed down off her sides and obscured everything. In Fog Bay, as we called it, the temperature rose from unbearable to merely bitter and we found ourselves contending instead with visibility so bad that we did not dare relay, for fear of losing one sledge while hauling the other. Fortunately, we found that once more it was possible to pull them both together. After a night of heavy snow, we needed two hours, in addition to all the usual work, just for digging out the tent and the sledges. But even on the new snow, we made a distance that should have seemed normal and instead struck us as nigh on miraculous: eight miles!

●–●–●

Amid danger and bleakness, it is funny what will comfort you. Imagine standing in darkness so profound you might think for a moment that you are locked in a frozen barn. Gradually, as your eyes adjust, you sense rather than see that there is sky

---

*Bill managed to understate the conditions he had experienced while returning from Cape Crozier in October 1903, which were about the same. Amundsen had also experienced these temperatures near the North Magnetic Pole.

above you. There is a faint pall caused by starlight. A bit of squinting reveals that the ground is grey (snow!) and the various other shapes (Mount Terror to the left?) are distinguished by being a deeper shade of black. It takes ten minutes of fiddling with the matches to get one quick glance at the compass. But now you notice directly ahead of you a yellow light, like the lamp of a solitary rambler seen from miles away across a desolate moorland. It could be a star, almost, but it is bigger than any star. You don't need the compass now: Jupiter has risen!

The Antarctic sky is a confusing place to an Englishman. Nearly all the familiar stars are missing, and the few familiar constellations are upside down. Worst of all, instead of rising in the east and setting in the west, the whole shooting match revolves from right to left around the horizon, like the lights on a carousel. But, as we eked our way east towards Cape Crozier and the days turned into weeks, Jupiter never failed us. At eight every morning, he would be sitting exactly on the horizon at exactly due south. As the morning wore on, he would rise a couple of degrees and shift slightly east. By three or four in the afternoon, he was five degrees above the horizon to the northeast, our exact direction of travel. All I could see of him, sans spectacles, was a yellow smudge, but even that was distinctive, unmistakable. Having Jupiter there was like climbing high on a cliff at night, fearing the abyss below but always being able to reach up and find one sure handhold.

●━●━●

By this time our sleeping bags were just like our finnesko, only bigger and therefore worse. Because the air at night was too cold to breathe, we slept—if only that were the right word!—with the bags closed tight over our heads. More damp with every breath, more ice, more weight. Then, when we had rolled them and put them on the sledge, they froze solid. Each night we had to fight our way into these giant snail shells a few inches at a time, kicking and shivering violently until enough of the ice melted to make them pliable.

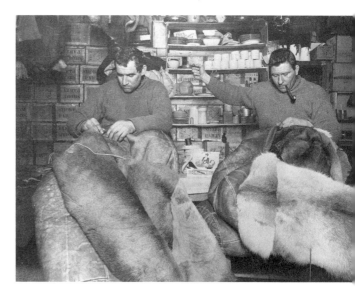

Tom Crean and Taff Evans mending reindeer sleeping bags shortly before the Winter Journey

Bill and I started the trip with the fur of our bags on the inside. It took only a few days for me to change my mind and follow Birdie's fur-outside example; Bill did the same a week later. Then Birdie, just to be contrary, switched to fur inside. Ponko wrote a poem explaining this important subject:

> *On the outside grows the furside, on the inside grows the*
> *   skinside;*
> *So the furside is the outside, and the skinside is the inside . . .*

The fashion in sleeping-bag arrangements continued to change for nearly three weeks as we slogged our way to Cape Crozier. (After that, the bags split so badly and accumulated so much ice that reversing them became impossible.) Whatever side the fur side, my bag was too big for me. Given all the hours I spent in it, I must have slept sometimes, but I don't remember sleeping. What I remember, six or seven hours a night, is a desperate and futile effort to warm up to a point where sleep might be possible. As I lay there clutching myself, or rocking back and forth, or kicking my legs up and down, I took perverse comfort from the sound of Birdie snoring and the sound of Bill humming hymns to himself. My teeth did not chatter in those temperatures. My body chattered. And then, suddenly and involuntarily, it would thrash, like a snake on a stick, until I thought my back would break. Finally, just about the time I thought I might be drifting off, or perhaps it was just after I really had drifted off, Bill would bellow, in his falsetto imitation of the landlady at a country inn, "Breakfast time, gentlemen! Rouse ye'shelves! Breakfast time!" It was only a joke, but it seemed a cruel one. Every morning, it made me think of porridge and kippers and bacon and eggs, but not enough to make our pemmican and biscuit taste like them.

❤❤❤

On the morning of Sunday, 9 July, we were still wrapped in fog. After two hours of slavery, during which I felt that each sledge must weigh a thousand pounds, we realized why it was so hard: we were moving uphill. No mistake had been made. We were beginning to cross the end of Terror Point, just as we had planned to do. But in poor visibility, with no landmarks, we had not been able to detect the gradient beneath our feet.

I remember that first day on Terror Point because Bill kept saying how much harder it was than he could have known. He was not complaining, for I never heard Bill complain about anything, ever. He was apologising. He was offering us the opportunity to say "Bill, this is madness. We need to turn back."

Let me be frank: I would have loved to turn back. I was colder than I had ever imagined possible, wracked by a constant, nagging hunger, and tired in every fibre. Yet I knew how much Bill wanted to reach Cape Crozier and find those penguins. As for Birdie, I knew that if both his legs froze solid and fell off, he would drop to his elbows and crawl there. I might have resented their strength, I might have felt belittled by it, but I did not. Mostly, being with them made me feel indestructible. Much to my surprise, I found that I wanted to keep going, too.

●●●

We heard the Pressure before we saw it. Windless Bight and the slopes of Mount Terror were eerily silent. But farther east, where the Barrier actively presses up against the obstacle of Ross Island, was an area that never stopped talking. The ice ridges popped, wheezed, grunted, and wailed in a manner about which it was not easy to feel calm. They even sang sometimes, like distant wind.

Still, the sounds were as nothing compared to the effect on one's nerves of travelling blind through an area webbed with crevasses. I fell into these bottomless traps several times. Once or twice, I caught myself and only went in up to the waist.

Once, I was left dangling in space at the end of my sledging harness until Bill and Birdie managed to haul me up. For half an hour afterwards, I was too shaken to speak, except to squeak "Oh yes, fine, fine" in response to Bill's enquiries.

Bill recalled that in this area there was a narrow path of flat snow running between Ross Island and the Pressure. For three days we struggled on across the shoulder of the mountain, making agonisingly small daily distances as we tried to find that path. When the going became too ridged and broken, we veered a little to the north, onto the shoulder of the island; when it became too steep and rocky, we veered a little to the east, into the ice. It was not a very successful waltz, and on 12 July we had to go farther east anyway, into a mad jumble of blocks, ridges, and chasms.

● ● ●

It was warmer now, and two days into the Pressure a blizzard raised the temperature again, this time to a tropical +9°F. But the wind was so strong we could not leave the tent. Fortunately, we became warm enough in our sodden bags for sleep to find us again. When the storm broke, everything froze solid, but the temperature was ideal for sledging and we made eight miles.

The moon had a wonderful sense of timing that day. At one point we were running slightly downhill. We knew we were coming to the end of the Pressure. Perhaps we were getting careless. Anyway, the sledges for once kept nipping at our heels. It was hard to maintain a sensible pace, if any pace can be described as sensible when one is pulling sledges through an uncharted crevasse field in the dark. There was almost no light—and then the clouds parted just long enough for a shaft of moonlight to reveal a black chasm ten paces ahead of us. Had the moon shone through five seconds later, it would have lit up the soles of our feet as we plummeted headlong to our deaths. We pulled up just in time.

That night we had little opportunity to dwell on our close call. Over our evening meal a new fear set in: we were becoming critically short of fuel. Because of the intense cold, we had been letting the cooker go for a few minutes every night after the meal; now we shut it down as soon as the food was warm. I lay in my ice-laden bag shivering violently, unable to get warm. Perhaps it was partly the shock of our narrow escape. I don't believe I slept at all.

The next day was clear. Mount Terror loomed above us. Now we could dimly make out our destination, the Knoll, a 1,200-foot cinder cone on Terror's eastern flank, standing sentinel over the cliffs at Cape Crozier. It took most of the morning to break camp. For much of the afternoon, we had to use crampons* over our finnesko to haul ourselves up a 700-foot rise, where the surface was old snow that might as well have been polished iron.

But we were there! After nineteen days of pulling, and trying to keep one another cheerful, and privately dreaming about the infinite cosiness of being dead, we had arrived in the land of the Emperors.

---

*The crampons were simply leather soles with two spiked metal plates at toe and heel; they attached to the finnesko by means of straps.

6

EGGS

CAPE CROZIER, LATE JULY 1911

I HAD BEEN standing there for several minutes, scraping my lenses clear and then thirstily taking in the scene before the ice crystals obliterated everything again. Bill crunched down the slope and stood beside me for a long time in silence. Then he put his hand on my shoulder in his fatherly way.

"Funny, isn't it," he said, "how even the ghastly places are beautiful."

"From what I can see," I replied, "the ghastly places are the most beautiful of all."

Bill chuckled. "With an attitude like that, Cherry, you should consider becoming an explorer."

We were standing on a slight rise just below the tent, with Mount Terror behind us. Looking down the slope to our right, we could see the all-too-familiar Pressure, deep creases stretching away to the southeast like furrows in a ploughed field, and beyond them, riding the southern horizon, faithful Jupiter. In front of us, a clear line divided the white of the Barrier from the white of the frozen sea.

The three most inconvenient eggs in the history of ornithology

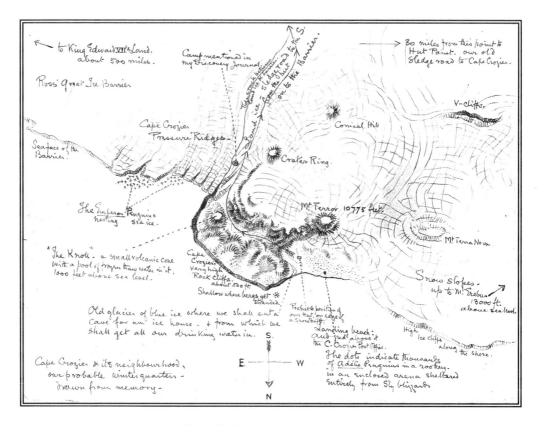

The map contains the following handwritten annotations:

← to King Edward VII's Land. about 500 miles.

Ross' great Ice Barrier.

Camp mentioned in my Discovery Journal.

→ 30 miles from this point to Hut Point. our old Sledge road to Cape Crozier.

V-cliffs.

Cape Crozier Pressure Ridges—

Conical Hill

Seaface of the Barrier.

Crater Ring.

The Emperor Penguins nesting sea ice.

Mt Terror 10775 feet.

Mt Terra Nova

"The Knoll" a small volcanic cone with a pool of frozen thaw water in it. 1000 feet above sea level.

Cape Crozier very high Rock cliffs. about 500 ft. Shallow where bergs get stranded.

Probable position of our Hut, on edge of a Snowdrift.

Snow slopes up to Mt Erebus. 13000 ft. above sea level.

Old glacier of blue ice where we shall cut a Cave for an ice house. + from which we shall get all our drinking water in.

Landing beach: and just above it the C. Crozier Post Office.

High Ice cliffs along the shore.

The dots indicate thousands of Adélie Penguins in a rookery. in an enclosed arena sheltered entirely from S'ly blizzards

Cape Crozier & its neighbourhood, our probable Winter quarters - drawn from memory -

S.
E.   W
N

Bill's map of Cape Crozier, drawn from memory after the Discovery expedition. Oriana Hut was just southwest of the Knoll in the direction of the Crater Ring

Finally Bill clapped me gently on the back, which was perhaps his way of saying that, however hard we had been working, there was more to do. And indeed we had barely turned round when a mocking voice hailed us from farther up the slope: "Are you ladies planning to pick flowers down there all morning?"

Laughing at the joke, or at the absurdity of anyone having a sense of humour at all in a place like this, we trudged back up to where Birdie was piling rocks.

We had intended from the start to build something stronger and warmer than our canvas tent at Cape Crozier. A short exploration showed that loose rocks were more abundant higher up the slope. The area was also just below the lip of a ridge, which Bill said would protect us against the wind. He turned out to be spectacularly wrong about the wind, but it seemed like good advice at the time. We started building the "igloo" there.

It wasn't really an igloo at all. It was more or less rectangular, for one thing, and it had stone walls and a canvas roof. We used ice only to strengthen and insulate it. Birdie, easily the strongest, was chief rock shifter. Bill and I accepted his deliveries of granite, basalt, and lava, and did the actual building. This was a good arrangement, since the heaviest rocks that Birdie could hack from the ice and carry a hundred yards were ones that I, with great effort, could barely pick up.

After a whole day's work, we were far from done, but it was Bill's tenth wedding anniversary and we decided that this was a fine excuse to go ahead and christen the structure anyway. "I name this magnificent edifice Oriana Hut," said Birdie, smacking a ball of snow against it in place of the traditional champagne bottle. Oriana Wilson, safe at home in England, would have felt more honoured by the thought than by the architecture. Even when completed, the "magnificent edifice" was nothing but a crude wall of stones, held together with snow and topped by a sheet of canvas. It didn't look as if we were building. It looked as if we were doing archaeology at a Neolithic ruin.

And our ruin was to stay ruinous for a while yet. Soon after our little ceremony, the wind came down upon us with fantastic violence, as if the hand of God had arrived to press the world flat. We had to abandon the site and retreat to the tent for the whole day; there, although the thermometer read a "mere" –25°F, our enforced idleness made us feel much colder.

At last the wind relented, which is to say that it dwindled to what any normal person would describe as a gale, but by that time a different worry kept us from further building. We were dangerously short of oil, having already started the fifth of our six cans. We had come to study the penguins, but now they would also have to keep us alive. We needed their blubber for fuel.

Getting to the rookery looked easy at first. Having to pack only one sledge, and that with just the essential scientific gear, made a big difference to the scale of the morning chores, and we were away by 9.30 A.M., picking our way down an icy slope towards the point where the Pressure butted up against the island. Bill's idea was to go downhill to the east and then turn north and cut in under the cliffs onto the sea ice.

All fine for the first hour. But we soon came into a maze of deep ridges. For two hours we blundered about in them, unable to see far in any direction. Sixty-foot mounds of loose ice hung above us, while weak snow bridges kept collapsing at our feet. Worst of all, or best of all (I cannot say which), we got to a point where our path was blocked by another impassable wall of ice and we could hear a distant, mournful honking. It made me think of elderly men trying to play in a dance band, without quite enough puff to get clean notes from their trumpets. So near and yet so inaccessible . . . the Emperors!

"Perhaps we could get to them by going this way," Bill said after a couple of minutes, gesturing with his ice axe. He took three steps to the left, holding up his lamp, then leapt back with a gasp as a crust of snow disintegrated beneath him, unveiling an ugly blue-black chasm. We gave it up at that point. Two hours later, more by luck than by judgement, we had clawed our way out of the Pressure and back to the tent. No penguins. No blubber. So once more we ate our dinner in the dark, wondering how many more hot meals we would live to taste.

Our evening meal was the same, night after night. A thin "hoosh," or stew, made from pemmican and water, biscuits, a small ration of butter, and a nice mug of hot water.* Sometimes, for variety, Bill would melt his butter into his hot water, instead of eating it whole or melting it into the hoosh. But I liked my water just the way it was. That cascade of inner warmth was like a magical spell, and I was so eager not to waste the heat that I repeatedly scorched my lips on the battered aluminium mug.

At least we got to sleep early. Either that or the underlying sense of panic must explain why we were up by 3 A.M. getting the igloo finished. Birdie went at it with a frenzy, shifting rocks and shovelling ice like Hercules at work in the stables of Augeas. Bill and I kept up with him as best we could, though we had eaten no breakfast and it was grim labour on an empty stomach. By the light of the hurricane lamp, we laid one sledge across the top of our rough wall, as a sort of roof beam, then fitted the canvas roof over that, carefully locking it down at the edges with large stones.

---

*Tea was on the menu only at breakfast and lunch. It was, by the way, "South Pole Tea," blended for the expedition by Cooper, Cooper and Company.

At last, we stopped to eat. Then, in the first hint of thin grey light, we headed out for our second assault on the rookery.

This time, we looked around us much more carefully on the way down the slope. Birdie spotted an opening we had not seen before, which turned out to be a way in under the cliffs. To our horror, though, it led to a narrow ledge, with a forty-foot drop to the Barrier on one side and yet another unfathomed crevasse on the other. We cached the sledge, took only a couple of knives and the Alpine rope, and crawled across, knees athwart the sides, like caterpillars on a twig.

At the other end, another wall of ice stood in our way. I was just steeling myself to crawl back the way we had come when Birdie discovered a sort of rabbit hole, too small for the sledge but just wide enough for us to wriggle through. On the other side, we found an easy scramble over some large blocks of ice that took us almost all the way down.

❤❤❤

From here we could see a huddle of black shapes against the white plain below us. We crouched there, silent as ghosts, for a minute that seemed like an hour. Bill shuffled closer and squatted down beside me.

"Can you see them, Cherry?" he whispered.

"Yes!"

"Take a good long look, O my Assistant Zoologist. Those are nesting Emperor penguins. We are the first men ever to see this."

Stirring stuff, though actually I could see so little that the penguins, shifting obscurely in the dim light, might have been dancing the can-can for all I knew. In any case, there was no time to savour the moment. The dim midday twilight was already beginning to fail, and we were still a dozen feet above the rookery. The final distance was a sheer drop. Just enough so that if we all went down, we would never climb up again. Much as we admired the Emperors, none of us wanted to become one.

The Emperors of Cape Crozier nursing their chicks on the sea ice beneath the cliffs, as drawn by Bill during daylight, September 1903

"We need a pair of strong arms up here," Bill said to me. "What we need down there is sharp eyes."

"It's all right," I said, in a tone that I hoped sounded casual and business-like, though it was bitterly disappointing not to go those last few feet. I braced myself in the snow, the Alpine rope about my waist, and lowered Bill and Birdie onto the edge of the frozen sea.

As they disappeared over the side, their voices shredded by the wind and their bodies dissolving into the mist and darkness, I realised that I was more alone, here at the extreme edge of this uninhabited continent, than I ever had been or ever would be. I might as well have been the last man on earth. To my surprise, it was a pleasant feeling. I thought: If I were to die, this would not be a bad place. I felt humbled by bearing witness to this biological miracle in a place so forsaken, so unforgiving. Still, I was not sorry when, after only fifteen minutes, a cheery shout woke me from my reverie: "Hullo-o! Anybody up there want to buy a penguin?"

The voice might have come from half a mile away, except that it was accompanied by three jerks on the rope. I stood up at once, braced my legs, and bawled "Ready!"

The first load was easy: a single fur mitten filled with six precious eggs, each one the size of a squashed tennis ball. The mitt was followed by three Emperor penguin carcases. Now the Emperor penguin is a substantial bird, and these fifty-pound cylinders of fat and feather had to come up one at a time. I stacked them pyramid-fashion, like big pieces of firewood. "Sorry, chaps," I muttered. "It was you or us."

My shoulders were already feeling that they had had quite enough, but now I had to bring up the humans. Bill came first; to my surprise, after a spot of bother with a snarled rope, he popped up easily, chattering away as if he had just come back from feeding the ducks in Kensington Gardens.

"Bloody marvellous, Cherry! Just like an army of irritable old biddies at a church fête. They weren't a bit afraid. One of them came right up to me, bold as brass, and pecked my trousers! I felt a dreadful cad, though. If you're going to kill an animal, you expect to have to chase it."

Getting Birdie up from the rookery was not so simple, even with two of us to do the pulling. He had put his right leg through some rotten ice and it was frozen solid from hip to toe, so there was very little he could do to help us. Eventually, after Bill and I had put in a series of heaves and grunts, he slithered onto the ledge—"Sorry about that!"—and started up his own commentary.

"Tremendous lot of them, right out to the sea edge. Hundreds, wouldn't you say, Bill?"

"Well, perhaps a hundred or so. But nothing like as many as I saw here before."

"Comical fellows, though. Didn't know what to make of us at all. They don't seem to have nests. They just waddle around with the eggs balanced on their feet. Most of them were in a big huddle, but there were others at the edge just poking about and squawking, as if they had had their membership of the club revoked." He put his hand on one of our three victims: "Ruddy big, too."

Bill laughed. "I think some of them were nearly as tall as you, Birdie."

After that, our way back to camp was quite swift. Or perhaps I should say too swift. We distributed the eggs so that each was protected by the warmth of a mittened hand, but I clumsily broke both of mine when I stumbled over an unseen ice block. The one good thing about this was the discovery that crushed penguin egg is a fine lubricant for leather. After the mishap, my mittens smelled revolting whenever they thawed, but at least they were more pliable when they froze again.*

We collapsed gratefully into the shelter of the igloo, and soon a new triumph was recorded for the legendary Bowers metabolism. Despite its frigid bath, his leg thawed quickly and was not frost-bitten at all.

That should have been that: enough adventure for one

---

*Two eggs were broken that day on the way back to the igloo. Another one must have been smashed or lost during the events of the next two days, because only three survived the trip back to Cape Evans.

day! But Bill, who had skinned one of the penguins and started a fire on the blubber stove, was too enthusiastic about our new source of warmth and allowed the blubber to over-heat. When he leaned forward to peer at our fresh Emperor penguin steaks, the Most Primitive Birds in the World got their revenge. A nut-sized gob of the blubber leapt from the cooker into Bill's eye.

The pain must have been both intense and prolonged: he howled like a wolf. I had come to think of Uncle Bill as invin-cible, which made it all the more disturbing to see him pushed to the limit. Even after we had packed the burn with ice and helped him into his bag, his groans continued into the night.*

Towards morning I must have slept. When I opened my eyes, Birdie was bustling at the cooker, Bill was sitting up in his bag, and everywhere there was a roaring noise fit to wake the dead. One side of Bill's face was bloated, the eye swollen shut. But the other side was decorated with the familiar grin. "Still alive!" he shouted. "Can't see a thing, but I'm beginning to think it will be all right."

"The roof won't be all right if this keeps up," said Birdie. That was when I noticed the canvas above us. You might have

---

*It is worth noting what Bill said—and did not say—about the experience of be-ing nearly blinded by boiling fat. In his private diary, he wrote a single sentence about it: "Slept for the first time in our stone hut, and it was a bad one for me as I got a spirt [*sic*] of boiling oil in my eye and it gave great pain for many hours." In the first draft of his official report to Scott, he reduced this to "At this meal I had the misfortune to get some hot blubber sputtered in my eye." But the word *misfortune* was clearly too strong for him; he scratched the sentence out, and the final, printed version reads: "I was incapacitated for the time being by a sputter of the hot oil catching me in one eye."

expected it to be pressed inwards by the wind. Instead, it was being sucked upwards, forming a taut dome.

Bill followed my gaze. "I think it's because we built too close to the ridge," he shouted. "The wind is coming from behind us. It hits the ridge and is forced up. Creates a low-pressure area directly above. Next time we come here on holiday, remind me to build this bloody thing farther down the slope."

"Yes," said Birdie, "and next time don't forget the deck chairs."

Not only did the strange phenomenon of the negative pressure threaten to slurp us into the heavens, but it also sucked warm air out of the igloo and sucked everything else in. The igloo became even colder than the tent, and by that afternoon, despite an endless stuffing of cracks with snowballs, there was a three-inch drift of white powder and dark grey lava dust over everything. For a change of scenery, we staggered down the hill and moved the tent, which we now used for storing our extra gear, up into the lee of the igloo.

We barely slept that night. By Saturday morning, the wind had grown even louder. Sometime early that morning we also heard a sudden *thud thud thud*, as if some observer of our plight had clapped derisively and then stopped. I could not make sense of it, but Birdie must have known at once. He leapt for the exit, stood upright in the midst of the gale, and then, without so much as putting his head back inside, shouted, "Back in a minute!"

Bill was still in no fit state for heroics. "Stay here," I said as I scrambled out, intent on catching up with Birdie before he vanished into the swirling ice. Then it dawned on me. The tent was gone, swept away by the wind.

At first I was too focussed on catching up with Birdie—and too focussed after that on a monumental battle to retrieve whatever we had left in or around the tent—to think what this meant. Only as we brushed off the snow and reported back to Bill did the full horror of losing the tent dawn on me.

We were like shipwreck victims, on an island far out to sea. That sheet of canvas, with its bamboo poles, was our raft. With it, we might conceivably have returned safely across the cold ocean of Windless Bight. Without it, we could not.

We were dead now.

Well, in the interest of honesty, I should record that we did not all think we were dead, or did not all speak as if we thought so. After a long silence, Uncle Bill said, "Cheer up, chaps. We're not done for yet. Still got the spare floor-cloth." (Here he pointed a thumb at our straining roof.) "We can dig snow holes in the Barrier on the way back. Use this as a roof again. Warmer than the tent, probably."

This is what made Bill a leader, I suppose. The rational

Where not to build a shelter: Bill's sketch of Oriana Hut, the slope on which it was built, and the wind

man sees that disaster is inevitable, and dies. The irrationally optimistic man cannot see it, refuses to see the evidence at all, and therefore, by some paradox, it cannot see him. Disaster misses its mark, and he survives.

This idea cheered me a little, but it did not persuade me that Bill was right. When I saw in my mind's eye that space in the snow where the tent had been, I accepted that there was no chance at all. I even found myself smiling at the irony: waiting at the rookery, I had indulged the idea that this would be a pleasant place to die. Now I would get to find out.

Nothing much should have mattered after that. But a dying man still feels hunger, and it seemed a cruel blow when, that same evening, the intense heat of the burning blubber melted the stove's feed pipe halfway through our attempts to prepare dinner. The whole apparatus was now useless.

●●●

When I awoke on Sunday morning, 23 July, I should have felt that death was not merely inevitable but imminent, too. Yet the mind is a funny thing. Because we had the shelter of the igloo and because our supplies of biscuit meant that we would not immediately starve, we lingered in a kind of fantasy state. While part of my mind accepted death, another part refused to look into the future. Right now, *right now*, everything was all right. Therefore, the logic seemed to go, everything would always be all right. It was as if I could go on living after all, provided I was careful about living only in the present moment.

At least we had something to celebrate. Through a lid still cracked and swollen, Bill discovered that his eye had suffered no permanent damage.

"Do I look frightful?" he asked, in mock concern.

"A disgrace to the whole expedition," said Birdie. "Count your blessings that Ponko isn't here."

This light banter, which had occurred during a lull in the wind, did not last long. Towards noon, with the monster over our heads fiercer and hungrier than ever, we started to notice that the sucking effect was increasing. Or else the canvas was stretching. We were sure that the edges of the canvas, tightly packed in around the sides of the igloo, had not moved, but every hour the dome rose another half inch clear of the sledge on which it was supposedly resting. The wind was now Force 11, according to Birdie: about 65 to 70 miles per hour, or a little less than a full hurricane. Birdie, though, was a man so steeled against the sin of exaggeration that he underestimated everything. Let me follow his example, then: it was windy.

When the calamity finally happened, Birdie was crouched by the entrance, stuffing snow (or socks, or pats of butter for all I know) into one of the cracks. I happened to look up just as a tear appeared in the canvas above his head. Half a second later, there was a noise like God ripping the sky in half, and the effect was what one would expect if a barrel of gunpowder had gone off on top of the sledge. In an instant, the entire canvas was reduced to a dozen ragged streamers. The sky opened above us, and the wind conspired with gravity to pile in on top of us great walls of icy snow that had accumu-

How Cold Was It?

Water freezes at +32°F (0°C).

Above +20°F sledging is difficult because the surface is too soft.

Between +15°F and −20°F is the ideal range for sledging, if the weather is calm. But a moderate breeze at the lower end of this range makes the "effective temperature" −50°F or less. At this temperature, exposed flesh freezes in under five minutes.

Below −25°F sledging is difficult because the snow forms hard, "sandy" grains that do not melt under the runners. Even in the middle of this range, a moderate breeze makes for an "effective temperature" of −70°F. In these conditions, exposed flesh freezes almost instantly.

Actual midday temperature in still air, 6 July 1911, Windless Bight: −77½°F (109°F below freezing)

°F	°C
30	−1
20	−6
10	−12
0	−17
−10	−23
−20	−28
−30	−34
−40	−40
−50	−45
−60	−50
−70	−56
−80	−62

lated around the igloo, as well as several large chunks of the wall itself.

Birdie leapt into his bag. Plenty of snow beat him to it, but he squirmed in anyway. Then all three of us instinctively rolled over so that the undersides of the bags were uppermost and we were lying on the flaps. The shredded remains of the roof were making a noise like a party of drunkards at a firing range.

A few minutes later I could tell that Bill was bellowing at the top of his lungs, but I still barely heard him say "Are you all right?"

Yes, we replied, yes we're all right, which was true in the narrow sense that we were not actually dead. Oddly enough, I found that I was comfortable. The layer of snow on top of my bag kept me warm. I was hungry but not yet painfully so. And there was no urgency to our situation, for the simple reason that there was nothing we could do about it.

It was in that state that regret and self-pity came visiting at last. What a bloody fool I had been, wasting so much of my life! Why, oh why, could I not have my years back and make more of them? Failing that, could I not be allowed to eat tinned peaches in syrup one more time? Failing even that, oh, please please please, could I have a quick death? For death itself seemed a grand idea. I did not fear Shakespeare's "undiscovered country from whose bourn no traveller returns." I feared only that getting there would involve pain.

Thus we lay in our bags under the snow, framed by the ruin of a stone hut, waiting for the end. Whenever the wind relented a little, Birdie, who was in the middle, would thump us both to see if we were still alive. Then we would sing a verse or two of a hymn.

Towards evening, Bill suddenly laughed out loud. "I think," he said, "that this is the funniest birthday I have ever spent!"

We had forgotten. He was thirty-nine years old.

7

A LONG WAY HOME

CAPE CROZIER TO CAPE EVANS,
JULY TO AUGUST 1911

I HAVE SO many memories of the couple of days after we lost the igloo roof, and each one is vivid, pungent, distinct. Yet they are smeared and tangled together like strands of wool. I cannot put them in order.

I do remember the wind's final insult, which was to tumble the sledge down on top of us. It was empty, and cushioned by a foot of snow, so we let it lie there. I even derived some comfort from the idea that now, at least, I and my bag could not be blown away.

Three hunched figures in the middle of the night (Bill's painting)

At one point the wind subsided to a mere breeze, and we stumbled about in the dark, hoping to find the tent. My wet clothes stiffened and froze almost immediately. I was happy to give it up, get back into the bag, and lie there, smugly getting almost warm again. This state lasted until I realised that Birdie had somehow managed to move the sledge, clear a space in the snow, partially mend the cooker, and prepare our first hoosh in forty-eight hours.

Did the hoosh and the tea take so long because the cooker

was broken or because we had so little fuel? Or did it not take long but only seem to? All I know is that both items on the menu were seasoned with reindeer fur, penguin feathers, and dirt, that the flavour of the day was burnt penguin blubber, and that it tasted almost magically delightful.

At some point, a thin grey light began leaking across the northern heavens and turned by degrees into a true glow, the brightest we had seen all winter. Instantly Birdie had his finnesko on and was up and about. Somewhat less instantly, Bill and I struggled out of our bags with the idea that, for form's sake, perhaps we should join him.

"See what I can find," Birdie muttered as he charged off into the swirling drift. In a moment of misunderstanding, I hesitated to follow, thinking this might be a polite way of saying that he needed to take care of his essential bodily functions. "See what I can find" indeed! What Birdie found was simply a miracle.

He had been gone several minutes by the time Bill and I finished batting crusts of ice from our clothes. We set off after him and almost immediately heard a shout from below. Staggering in the direction of the sound, we both slipped, both slid, and both ended up travelling on our bottoms—excellent for speed though less so for dignity—to the very point where Birdie was standing over his glorious, glorious prize.

It had been ripped from our campsite and hurled into the sea two days before. Its disappearance had signed our death warrants: without it, we had no hope. And yet incredibly, against all sane odds, it was not in the sea. It was here, caught in a hollow at the bottom of a gully. A thing of infinite beauty.

A greasy piece of green canvas. The tent! And apparently the wind had sucked the canvas shut as it rose, like an umbrella, for although two of the poles were broken, they were still intact and still attached.

Bill shook his head from side to side, like a man who admits that a difficult puzzle in the back of the newspaper has defeated him. How could this be? After fingering the canvas as one might touch a holy relic in a hard-to-find alcove at the back of a cathedral, he muttered, "It's not possible!"

I knew what he meant, but it *was* possible. It had happened. We had come back from the dead. In a reverential silence, we carried the tent back to where our bags lay and carefully secured it. Nobody spoke until we were once more inside that ruined igloo. I think only two things were said even then.

First Birdie: "This is an excellent turn. Now we can get ourselves sorted out and have another go at the rookery." Then Bill: "Birdie old man, you are a dear, dear chap, but you are perfectly mad. The time for ornithology is over. I am not prepared to risk your lives for one minute longer. We are going home."

Home. A thrilling idea, yet we found ourselves incapable of moving quickly. I don't know whether it was exhaustion, or cold, or just the shock of discovering that, instead of dying quietly in the snow, we would have to do more sledge-hauling in the process of saving ourselves. Whatever the reason, we broke camp even more slowly than usual. Bill and I made a cache of scientific gear in one corner of the hut while Birdie got the sledge ready. We left a note in a matchbox, attached to a pole, giving the date and stating that all was well. But when we did get moving, it was pitch-dark and windy. Even though we were leaving one sledge and much equipment behind, the wind had come back with a vengeance—Force 9 at least—and we managed to cover only a single mile before making camp again. We had not even got off the mountain and back into the Pressure.

●━●━●

Let me tell you something about duck down. In its natural state, duck down is attached to a duck's bottom. Underneath a waterproof casing of feathers, it stays dry and is one of nature's best insulators, a soft and almost weightless fortress against the cold.

Unfortunately, as ducks well know, down is useless when it gets wet. We had brought Eider down liners for our bags because Eider ducks are renowned, even among ducks, for having the most sumptuously insulated of all bottoms. But my liner was soaked, and it had come out of my sleeping bag when Bill and I scrambled to follow Birdie on his tent-hunting expedition. On our return, I found it in the snow, a dirty white mass that put me in mind of a dead sheep, or perhaps a child's papier-mâché model of the Alps. It was frozen solid.*

---

*The use of down liners inside the reindeer bags was one of several experimental innovations for the Cape Crozier journey. Scott correctly predicted, in his diary, that they would be helpful for a while and then rapidly become useless when wet.

"You're wasting your time with this," Birdie said, kicking the offending lump, and not for the first time, he offered me his own. It was still wrapped up, dry and pristine, on the sledge: incredibly, he had never used it. I felt terrible, but a starving man will accept food from a man who is merely hungry, especially when the merely hungry man looks you in the eye and claims not to be hungry at all. It's true that Birdie was in the best physical shape of any of us, not least because on some nights he was warm enough to sleep. Because of his precious gift, I, too, who felt that I might crack from sheer exhaustion, got several nights in a row of proper rest. Within a few days, alas, Birdie's liner had absorbed so much moisture from my bag that it also became almost useless.

That first night of our return journey, Birdie looped our rope around his bag and lashed it to the tent. "If this bally thing goes anywhere again," he said, "I'm going with it." Fortunately, although the wind clawed at us again all night, Birdie and the tent stayed put.

The sleeping bags, though, were wetter and more cracked than ever—Bill's had split all the way down one side—and we had to stop rolling them up in the mornings for fear that either they would disintegrate or we would never be able to get into them again. We took to laying them out full length on the sledge, flaps propped open, like a stack of coffins.

Back in the Pressure, we had almost no light, even at noon. We lost our way repeatedly. Meanwhile the temperature, responding as always to the absence of wind, dropped from the minus twenties into the minus forties. We kept wandering by mistake onto the lower slopes of Mount Terror and found our way back into the Pressure only to crash through snow bridges and narrowly avoid plunging in.

One of these occasions was more nearly fatal than the rest. Climbing an enormous ice ridge, at just the point where the Barrier meets the island, Bill put his foot through one edge of a snow bridge, and the remainder of the bridge fairly exploded under the feet of Birdie, who was just behind him. Bill had the hurricane lamp in his hand, and he spun it round to reveal a terrible sight. All around was white ice, except for a neat black hole and Birdie's head disappearing into it.

Birdie had fallen in because his headgear—an absurd green felt hat, with improvised nose flaps and earflaps, worn over a grey woollen Balaclava helmet—was too frozen for him to bend properly and see where he was putting his feet. Luckily, the crack was so narrow that he had been able to slow his fall by pushing outwards with his feet. But it was a near go for him: he kept sliding until his head was four feet below the surface. He was only loosely wedged, and the lantern revealed nothing but empty darkness beneath him.

I had cause to recall, at that moment, my own response to such an experience on the journey out. Birdie? Bill's words came back to me: "I don't think he knows what fear *is*." Our anxious cries of "Birdie! Birdie! Are you all right?" were met with a certain amount of muttering followed by "Bit tricky down here. Too narrow to move and the sides are too soft for me to get a foothold."

"What do you want us to do?"

"Make a bowline in the end of the rope, then feed it down to me slowly."

Trust a sailor to come up with a solution that involves a knotted loop in a rope! But Bill's fur mittens had vanished when the tent blew away; with nothing but dogskin gloves and woollen liners, his hands were in such bad shape that he could not tie the knot. I took over, getting my own fingers frost-bitten (again) in the process. But it's amazing how well the mind can be distracted from small matters, such as losing a few fingers, by the imminent death of a companion. "Hang on, almost done. Right, one bowline coming down."

"That's the ticket," Birdie said. "Right-o. I'm putting my foot into the loop. Now pull slowly on the loop. That's it. A bit more. Stop. Now pull on the harness . . ."

At last, the top of his hat came level with the surface. After one more heave on the rope, he flung out both arms and wriggled over the edge onto his belly, annoyed at himself for wasting time with such unnecessary acrobatics. And so it was that Birdie cheated death in a crevasse by calmly inventing a method of rescue that had, as far as I know, never been used before.

"Bracing down there," he said. "Carry on."

I watched Birdie carefully then, as he stood adjusting his mitten straps in the glow of the hurricane lamp. Was he just putting a brave face on things? Underneath it all, was he not

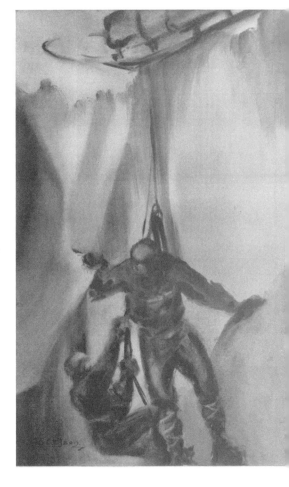

Down a crevasse— the only time to be glad that the sledge is heavier than you (Bill's painting)

just as shaken as any man would have been? I cannot be sure, but what I think is this: Birdie did know fear. Hunger, too, and cold and pain. But he also possessed an almost supernatural ability to stare them down. Ordinary men run from their worst experiences, or are engulfed by them; Birdie just looked them in the eye and said, "I'm too busy for you. Go away."

●—●—●

The light was improving every day. Soon after we left the Pressure and returned to Windless Bight, we could make out Castle Rock, a landmark on the Hut Point peninsula, just 25 miles distant to the southwest. At lunch on 29 July, Birdie's birthday, we looked back at our tracks and saw a spectacular conjunction: a sickle moon was scraping the northeast horizon, like a billowed sail cruising through the constellation Virgo, and just above it, like a light on the mast, was Venus.

Later that day, as we made camp, my foot went through a snow crust. This was not a crevasse but a broad "lid" of snow with an air space beneath it. Suddenly a vast area of this crust gave way, and with a series of booming noises the entire landscape around, including the tent and sledge, settled by nearly a foot. The noise of it went on for several minutes, and we stood there, frozen and appalled, until it came to an end.

The temperatures were still dreadful, but for sledging purposes the surface was better than before. We were making five, six, even seven miles a day, and it should have been an easy run back to safety. Yet we were so tired by now that Birdie and I, plodding together while Bill led in front, would fall asleep in the traces and wake when we bumped into each other. Our fuel was so critically short that we dared heat only two meals a day. We rued the fact that we had burned extra oil on the journey out in an attempt to warm ourselves. No chance of that now, and those nights of our return across the Barrier, marginally warmer according to Birdie's meticulous log, stand out in my memory as the most unbearably cold of all. Out of desperation, we had resorted to wearing our fur mittens inside our bags as we slept. Doing so kept our hands warmer; it also kept them permanently wet. They became pale white, almost translucent except for the red sores and black blistering, and so hideously shrivelled that they looked more like diseased jelly-fish than human hands.

One of the greatest comforts and greatest torments while we marched was thinking about warm rooms filled with food. As my body forced itself to take the next step, my mind would drift away to imaginary London restaurants. These places were always equipped with thundering log fires, and their tables were loaded with roast beef, generously buttered potatoes, and, inevitably, tinned peaches in syrup.

My mind went to those places because they brought relief, but the longer I spent there the greater was the agony of coming back. I would find myself wishing that my companions were a couple of soft, easily beaten men, because then we could all agree to lie down comfortably and die in the snow. For those bad moments, when my body was shrieking *Stop, Cherry, stop!* I invented a mantra. Ten times, or twenty, or a hundred, whatever it took to get over the bad moment, I would repeat to myself: "You've got it in the neck. Stick it!

Stick it! You've got it in the neck. Stick it! Stick it!" The siren calls of comfort and defeat never went away, or not for long, but my mantra made me feel that I was talking back, so the battle of mind over matter was not yet lost.

"You've got it in the neck. Stick it! Stick it!"

⬬⬬⬬

Our last full day on the Barrier, Sunday, 30 July, was a nightmare. Wreathed in pain, we slogged along in a temperature that felt much colder even than the thermometer's frightful –57°F. Yet I record these facts with pride: We did not lose our tempers. We did not blame one another for problems great or small. We did not forget to be polite.

The following afternoon, thank God, we saw a faint grey line in the distance and knew everything would be all right. The Barrier edge! We ran the sledge down a bank of snow onto the sea ice, stopped for a meal, and in no time at all were rounding Cape Armitage and digging out a snowdrift at the door of the old *Discovery* hut.

One more minor disappointment awaited us. We had hoped, dreamed, assumed that someone at Cape Evans would have sledged down and left dry sleeping bags, sugar, food. There was nothing. But at least the hut had a plentiful supply of oil, and I found myself half-choking with emotion at the sight of familiar objects: chairs, glass bottles, a stack of bright orange Huntley & Palmer biscuit tins. We also found a dry tent, left over from *Discovery* days, which we pitched inside the hut for extra insulation. One more night in those awful dripping bags, but we knew now that we were safe. We even got some extra rest, for in the morning the wind was too strong for us to leave. We stayed in the hut, nibbling biscuit, dozing, and talking with relish about the haircuts and clean clothes that would soon be ours.

At about eleven o'clock we set off. It was a clear day by then, and we were out of Ross Island's shadow at last. Although the sun would not show itself for another month, we found ourselves sledging for the first time in what one might reasonably describe as daylight. We had a late lunch at the Glacier Tongue as the light faded, then one final, five-hour slog through the darkness.

"Spread out!" Bill cried as we neared Cape Evans. He wanted them to see at once that three men were returning. But it was already late evening; nobody was about. So the Winter Journey (as it came to be known) ended on a comical note. Bill banged on the door and shouted "Anyone home?" After a pause, the door opened to reveal a sailor in pyjamas with a look of stupefied horror on his face. He stared at us as if we were wraiths, his jaw moving without a sound. I really thought, for a second, that he would simply close the door in our faces. Instead, without so much as addressing a word to us, he bellowed back over his shoulder:

"Good God! Here's the Cape Crozier party!"

●━●━●

Perhaps his reaction was not surprising. With my skin blackened from penguin grease and my head encased in ice, Ponko

Still alive, just. Bread and jam with a mug of tea, an hour after returning

admitted that I "did not look like anything human." Silas Wright, ever the scientist, would write in his diary that I resembled a walking block of the clear mineral selenite. Bill shared a cubicle with Teddy Evans, and while some kind soul undid my finnesko for me, I stood in a daze, dripping, and watched Teddy actually cut the clothes from Bill's body. After that we sat around one end of the wardroom table in dressing gowns, drinking cocoa and eating big, rough hunks of bread and jam. Ponko took a photograph, in which I admit we look a bit of a sight: you can even see that my fingers are swollen. While we munched our bread, the others just stood around grinning and gawping, unable to believe we were truly alive.

Even Scott was lost for words. "Well, look here," he kept saying. "By Jove"—and then he just shrugged and burst out laughing. I heard him say only one coherent thing, as I climbed into my bunk: "This is the hardest journey ever made."

Going to sleep under warm blankets in that safe, friendly hut felt like slipping quietly out of this world, through a doorway, into paradise. I slept, that night, for a thousand years.

8

VICTORY IN DEFEAT

ROSS ISLAND, THE BARRIER,
AND THE BEARDMORE GLACIER,
OCTOBER 1911 TO NOVEMBER 1912

IMAGINE DRAGGING A sledge from Paris to Rome and back. But with higher mountains in the middle, and fewer hotels.

So vast an undertaking as the Polar Journey is hard for the mind to grasp. On the hellish odyssey to Cape Crozier and back, we had logged 135 miles. Almost three times that distance, 379 miles, separated our base camp at Hut Point from the edge of the Antarctic continent. Then the next 109 after that involve a brutal climb over the Transantarctic Mountains, via one of the largest glaciers on earth. Finally, in the thin air of the Polar Plateau, most of which is at 10,000 feet, you have to go 312 miles more before you can plant your flag and take your pictures at the featureless, God-forsaken spot around which the world turns.* And that is the first half of the journey. I

Final stage: Taff Evans and Titus Oates following Bill and Captain Scott at 10,000 feet on the Polar Plateau, less than 100 miles from the Pole (Birdie took the picture)

---

*These distances, all in nautical miles, are from the detailed log kept by William Lashly in his diary. (To be precise: they are from Cape Evans to the Lower Gla-

went two-thirds of the way, as part of the support team, and came back. Bill and Birdie went all the way, with Scott, Titus Oates, and Taff Evans. They did not come back.

●—●—●

The night of our return from Cape Crozier, my ruined clothes lay in an angular heap near my bunk, like discarded armour. In the morning, even after some of the ice had formed a puddle on the floor, they weighed 24 pounds. More astonishing was my sleeping bag. According to Birdie's equipment list, my new bag had weighed 12 pounds and the Eider down liner another 4 pounds on the day we left Cape Evans. When Taylor and Atkinson unpacked our sledge, which we had left outside the hut, my bag plus Birdie's liner weighed 45 pounds. Making allowances for the quantity of reindeer fur that ended up in my tea, I had been "sleeping" in 15 pounds of bag and about 30 pounds of frozen breath.

For many days after returning, while we nursed our healing frostbites, we walked as if the floor of the hut were studded with razor blades. But we were ravenously hungry every two hours, which everyone took to be a good sign. Birdie recovered quickest. Within a couple of days, he was looking towards the next winter, discussing with Scott the logistics of mounting "another assault on the rookery." Scott

cier Depot, from the Lower Glacier Depot to the Upper Glacier Depot at Mount Darwin, and from Mount Darwin to the Pole.) They imply a total distance of 1,600 nautical, or 1,840 statute, miles.

played along, but I do not think he took the idea seriously for a minute. He knew how close he had come to losing us.

On 22 August, the sun supposedly returned, though the weather was so bad that nobody actually clapped eyes on it until three days later. We had a celebration anyway, and I presented Scott with the second issue of the *South Polar Times*, complete with poems and sketches that dressed our Cape Crozier journey in the soft fabric of comedy.*

Captain Scott at work on his journal

Then Scott gathered us together to share his plan of attack. It was a complicated business, involving separate support teams powered by motor, pony, and dog. On the way to New Zealand, Scott had discovered that his great Norwegian rival, Roald Amundsen, was also making an attempt on the Pole. "I will not race," Scott said firmly. "We will complete our programme as if Amundsen did not exist." This was easy to say, and I am certain Scott meant it. But I could see the strain it caused him, especially knowing that Amundsen was relying

---

*Birdie contributed a poem about Oriana Hut, entitled "This is the House that Cherry built." Frank Debenham wrote that it "must have been written by Bowers almost immediately after his return, at a time when an ordinary man would have been much too busy feeling himself to see if he was alive to think of making fun of his recent escape."

on dogs: the ponies, less resistant to cold, would have to start for the Pole later in the season. Anyway, Scott's plan was to have the motor sledges start first. Everyone would cross the Barrier. The dogs, which Scott suspected were not capable of climbing the Beardmore Glacier, would then return, while most of the men and perhaps some of the ponies would climb the glacier to the Polar Plateau. Four men chosen by Scott at the last moment would go for the Pole.*

I was out in the stables with Titus one day, and he had said, as usual, no more than ten words in an hour. I had not taken seriously the possibility that I would be on the final team, but suddenly he looked at me meaningfully and declared, "It's you or me for the Pole, Cherry."

I knew at once that he was right. The Cape Crozier journey had given me a reputation as a tough traveller. I had progressed from holding the status of expedition baby—a fondly

---

*Amundsen had set up a trip to the North Pole, but on hearing that Peary had beaten him to the mark, he changed his mind and secretly decided to go south—so secretly that his ship left the Norwegian capital under cover of darkness and his own men did not know their true destination until long after they had left. Many of Scott's men, and not a few Norwegians, were offended by what they saw as this "sneakiness." Titus Oates disagreed. Admiring Amundsen both for his ability and for the fact that he had not made a big public fuss about his expedition, he confided to his mother, "I personally don't see it as underhand to keep your mouth shut." As for Scott, he was probably annoyed at the sudden prospect of being beaten to the Pole, but more annoyed that it would now be seen as a race whether he liked it or not. Scott knew Amundsen's sole objective was the Pole, whereas Scott had neither wanted nor planned for that kind of expedition. In his private diary he would say only: "That this action is outside one's own code of honour is not necessarily to condemn it and under no conditions will I be betrayed into a public expression of opinion."

tolerated hanger-on—to being one of the handful from whom Scott would choose his final team. It unnerved me to recognise that I had both a reputation and the burden of living up to it.

The motor sledges left Cape Evans on 24 October, supposedly taking their large, heavy loads all the way across the Barrier to stock a depot at the foot of the Beardmore in preparation for the return journey. Instead they were in trouble from the outset, overheating even on the sea ice to Hut Point, and they broke down so frequently that they soon had to be abandoned. The more durable of the two reached barely a mile beyond Corner Camp. At a cost of £1,000 each (a sum which, as Titus muttered through clenched teeth, would have purchased several hundred dogs), they had taken us barely fifty miles. The four men tending the machines were actually grateful when the last one died, because it meant they could give up cursing them for being so unreliable. But they had been ordered to

THE POLAR JOURNEY

Statute Miles
50   0   50   100

Geographical Miles
50   0   50   100

South Pole
Last Depot
1½ Degree Depot

P L A T E A U

3 Degree Depot

Axel Heiberg Gl.

Upper Gl. Depot
Mt. Darwin

Beardmore Glacier

Middle Gl. Depot
The Cloudmaker

Lower Gl. Depot

Taff Evans died

Lower Barrier Depot

Middle Barrier Depot

B A R R I E R

Upper Barrier Depot

Oates died

Tent
One Ton Depot

Bluff Depot

Bluff

Corner Camp
White I.
Barrier Edge
Safety Camp

R O S S
Ross
Island
McMurdo
Sound

S E A

wait for us at 80°32' South; now they had to man-haul
800 pounds of supplies for another two weeks to reach that
latitude.*

The main pony teams had it much easier, at first. We left
Cape Evans late in the evening on 1 November, and had only
to ski, steer, and cajole while the ponies did the hauling. My
own charge, Michael, was a recalcitrant beast on his own but
quite happy to plod along without complaint if he had one of
his kind to follow. Once we got onto the Barrier, there were
several blizzards, when we could not move at all, yet we aver-

---

*Despite all this, Scott and others considered the motor sledges a success: they
were, after all, a radical experiment in a wholly new technology, and Scott had
shown that the basic idea worked even if the design needed improving. ("I am
still very confident of the possibility of motor traction, whilst realising that re-
liance cannot be placed on it in its present untried evolutionary state," he wrote.)
It was a perfect example of his overall approach, which was not to narrow the expedition down to one goal but to use it for as much experimentation as possible.

aged ten miles a day. Progress seemed easy to me after the
Winter Journey. No sledge to pull. Sunshine. Enough food. A
dry sleeping bag! I even had the honour of a small, rare natural phenomenon being named after me. On 14 November, as a
midnight march brought us close to One Ton Depot, I noticed a circular "ground rainbow" in the ice crystals in front of
me. The others noticed it, too, and Bill not only sketched it
but immediately christened it Garrard's Halo. It is, no doubt,
the only halo I shall ever have.

I was sharing Scott's tent at this stage. He had a fanatical
neatness and fussiness about detail, which irritated some of
the men but suited me. Making and breaking camp was easy
with everything so organised. And I appreciated how he
found ways to make the evening meal subtly different every
day. He even finessed the switching back and forth from tea to
cocoa, proudly combining the stimulus of one and the food
value of the other in an invention he christened "teaco."

But the ponies were in a bad state from the start of this journey: weak, ill, and far too cold despite the late departure. We switched to marching at night, because they found it easier to rest during the warmest part of the day and work during the coldest, yet several sickened and had to be put out of their misery. Two dog teams, led by Cecil Meares and Dimitri Gerof, were doing better, but Scott remained convinced by Shackleton's reports that we would never get the dogs through the ice chaos of the Beardmore. Once they had supplied us as far as the glacier, already much farther than Scott originally planned, he instructed Meares to turn back.*

Then, only thirteen miles from the foot of the glacier, we were trapped for days by a blizzard—and the worst thing about this one—oh, irony—was warmth. For the first time since our arrival in the South, Birdie's thermometer actually registered temperatures a degree or two *above* freezing! Great wads of snow pelted us from every direction and immediately melted. Drifts piled up outside the tents, thick and wet like mashed potato. Inside, our clothes and bags dripped like sponges. After days of waiting, and of being on short rations but nevertheless eating food that should have been kept for later, we dug out and readied the sledges. But the ponies could barely move in the thick slush, and it fell upon Titus, of all people, to finish them off with his pistol. Not one of them lived

---

*What the expedition experienced on its way up to the Polar Plateau suggests that Shackleton and Scott were right. By contrast, Amundsen got his dogs up the Axel Heiberg Glacier without difficulty. Some say this is because the Axel Heiberg is less difficult than the Beardmore; others say that is nonsense. A good example of how difficult it is to get at the truth in these matters.

to help us climb the great ice river that now confronted us.

Scott had planned the journey to the Pole around three main power sources. We knew the motor sledges had been an experiment, yet we hoped they might be strongest; they sickened and died first. The ponies, about which Shackleton had felt

Bill's drawing of a camp on the Barrier

so confident, went next, despite all Titus's care; the necessities of a harsh land dictated that one by one their meat was either fed to the dogs or stockpiled for us. From now on, the next stage being judged too difficult even for the dogs, our lives would depend on pushing beyond its design limits our only remaining transportation technology, the human leg.

❦

The Beardmore is a monster, wider at its narrowest point than the biggest glacier in Europe is long. The snow we found on its lower sections was so soft that we were pushing the sledges through it like ploughs. Then, higher up, the surface hardened into "blue ice" that looked and felt like polished steel: it was nearly impossible to get a foothold. Birdie, the great understater of difficulties, summed up the Beardmore in the privacy of his diary as "the most back-breaking work I have ever come up against."

At least the crevasses provided a distraction from the hard

On the monster's back: slogging up the Beardmore Glacier in deep snow

labour: they were everywhere, many of them hidden under half-rotted snow bridges. One night, Birdie found one lurking a single pace from the side of his tent. I wish he had not tested its depth by tossing in an empty oil can. The hollow, fading clatter seemed to go on forever. The sound haunts my memory still.

During the day you could spot a snow bridge, in theory, by tell-tale changes in the snow's texture. But our snow-goggles were always fogging up with sweat, so sledge leaders marched with their goggles off and endured long days of squinting at the radiant whiteness of the snow. The result was predictable: the special agony of snow-blindness. Teddy Evans described it as "like trying to pick up burning sand with your eyelids."

Four days before Christmas, we reached 85°15' South, at an altitude of 7,700 feet. This point, close under the shadow of Mount Darwin, is practically the top of the glacier, though the plateau continues to slope gradually upwards to more than 10,000 feet. We had now placed several hundred pounds of supplies in depots; the loads were that much lighter, and Scott decided it was time to reduce the party from twelve men with three sledges to eight men with two. Titus would be among those continuing, and I would not.

I felt frustrated, but I also felt at the time that it was the right decision. After the climb up the Beardmore, I was feeling thoroughly done up. Titus still seemed indestructible. Actually, this was an illusion: Titus was merely stoical, and he was being stoical right then about his left thigh, which a Boer soldier's bullet had smashed during a skirmish in South Africa ten years earlier. The wound had left him with a permanent limp. He never mentioned it, or the extraordinary heroism that had gone with it.* On the Beardmore, though, Titus confided to Atch that it was suddenly painful again. This information never reached the ear of Scott, who may also have been swayed by knowing that Titus was the better navigator.

Atch, Silas Wright, and Petty Officer Keohane were told to return with me. Offering our best wishes and camouflaging our hearts in jokes and bluster, we waved as the other eight

---

*On 5 March 1901, near the small town of Aberdeen in South Africa's Cape Colony, the young Lieutenant Oates and his men were surrounded by a much larger force. The Boer commander sent several notes ensuring their safety if only they would give in. Titus sent a note back: "We came here to fight, not to surrender." They all escaped with their lives, just, and the young officer who had nearly bled to death from his leg wound became known throughout the British Army as No Surrender Oates.

Companions on the First Returning Party: (from left) Silas Wright, Atch Atkinson, A.C.G., and Patrick Keohane

disappeared over the horizon. Then we turned back down the glacier. With no gallant little ponies to help us, but with the sun warming our faces, we stumbled northwards, reaching Hut Point a month later.

The two remaining teams consisted of Scott, Wilson, Oates, and Taff Evans on the first sledge, and Teddy Evans, Bowers, Lashly, and Crean on the second. Scott believed that his own team was pulling the strongest. But Birdie, the strongest man on the other sledge, was also the best navigator of all eight, and Scott needed him. It would have made perfect sense, with hindsight, to take Birdie as a replacement for Taff, who had cut his hand badly on the last day of the year while mending one of the sledges. But Scott did not know that Taff's injury was serious. Taff, like Titus, was probably hoping the trouble

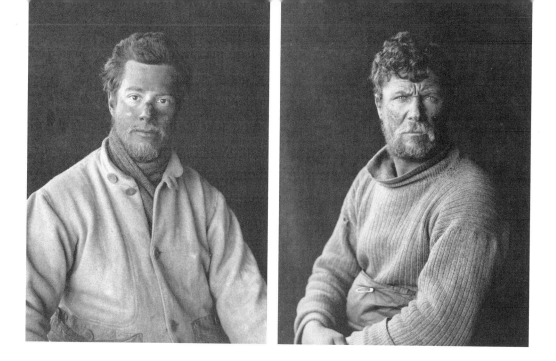

would go away quickly if he just kept quiet. Scott saw only two exceptionally fit and determined haulers. On 4 January, after two weeks of pulling on the Plateau, he made the fateful decision to add Birdie to his own party and continue with all five men.*

Everything had been planned for four. The food rations. The cooker. Even the size of the tent. Worse, Birdie's team had left their ski behind at one of the glacier depots, to save weight, so now the four taller men would ski to the Pole while

---

*Scott did not share his reasons for the change, but critics who imply that it was unplanned are clearly mistaken. He had been experimenting with five to a tent since the Depot Journey in February. Possibly, seeing that everyone was weakened by the struggle up the Beardmore, he believed that the Polar Party could succeed only with the pulling power of five men. In the end, the problem was not so much the number as the names: Crean and Wright should have replaced Evans and Oates. In retrospect, perhaps Scott should have demanded from Wilson a full medical examination of all the men and made his choice in the light of it.

December 1911, two days before Midsummer Day: a photograph taken at "night" near the top of the Beardmore, after a 23-mile climb. This was the camp from which the First Returning Party was instructed to turn back; it was also near the site where Bill found some of his best fossils on the return from the Pole. By Midsummer Day, the Polar Party had reached the Plateau

Birdie plodded beside them on his short legs.

It also meant that the Second Returning Party consisted of just three men: Petty Officer Tom Crean, Chief Stoker William Lashly, and Lieutenant Teddy Evans. Only Evans was a competent navigator; besides, a return with just three in the party was inherently more dangerous, because a bad injury to one would almost certainly be fatal to all three.

Surely enough, just about everything went wrong for them. Returning across the Plateau in a biting wind, they strayed several miles off course. They missed the entrance to the Beardmore and found themselves to one side of it, at the top of the Shackleton Ice Falls. An impassable barrier in any normal assessment, though they could see the glacier 2,000 feet below them. Evans believed they were already too short of food for a three-day detour around the Falls, so he ordered his men to face the near-suicidal alternative: they would get on the sledge and toboggan straight down. Lashly and Crean didn't want to do it, but they were used to following orders and probably guessed that in doing so they were choosing to have their brains dashed out rather than starve or freeze to death. At first they steered with their cramponed feet, then they lost control completely and the careening sledge reached 60 miles per hour before crashing into an ice ridge. They were bruised all over; their clothes were in shreds; by a miracle, none of them was seriously injured.

At the bottom of the Falls, however, their troubles were only just beginning. They found themselves in an area with crevasses "you could lose a cathedral in," as Lashly put it. One of these cut far across their path, and they had to cross it, using a narrow snow bridge that might have collapsed at any moment. Then, still on the glacier, Evans suffered a terrible bout of snow-blindness, followed immediately by a severe sickness of the stomach. By the time they reached the lower glacier, he was complaining of stiffness in the knees, and it occurred to Lashly that his boss was coming down with scurvy.

Evans soon became too weak to pull the sledge. By halfway across the Barrier, Lashly and Crean were helping him onto his ski. Shuffling alongside them, he made it to One Ton Depot, and fifty miles beyond, but on 14 February he could go no farther. Lashly and Crean threw away their ski, and nearly everything else except the little remaining food and the tent, and put Evans on the sledge. Then, on 16 February, already desperately hungry, they discovered that melting snow had leaked into and ruined most of their biscuit rations. Putting themselves on half rations, they dragged Evans the remaining fifty miles to Corner Camp.

Crean and Lashly were men cut from the same cloth as Birdie: quiet, efficient, indestructible. I think Scott had Lashly in mind, but it might have been any of these three, when he wrote in his diary, "It is splendid to have people who refuse to recognise difficulties."

And here forgive me for reducing to a paragraph one of

the most staggering acts of heroism in the history of exploration. While Lashly stayed in the tent to tend Evans, Crean put three sodden biscuits and two pieces of chocolate in his pocket and set out alone for Hut Point. It was 10 A.M. on Sunday, 18 February. The weather was fair, at first, but the snow was deep and a blizzard was chasing down out of the south. Crean walked west, directly into the area around the end of White Island, which is raked with crevasses. You never go into crevasse country alone: one fall and you die. Yet he had no choice. At least he had the advantage of travelling light, you might say: he had no ski, no goggles, no map nor even a bottle of water. He plunged on through the rising drift for thirty miles, stopping for five minutes at Observation Hill to eat the chocolate and some of the biscuit, and arrived at Hut Point at three o'clock on the Monday morning. He had been walking

for over seventeen hours. Atkinson fed him brandy followed by a bowl of porridge. He consumed both with relish, vomited them both up, and then volunteered to go straight back out with Atkinson to guide the rescue. But by then the blizzard had descended. Nobody was able to leave the Hut until late the next day.

Atkinson refused to let Crean go out again. Leaving him at the Hut, and with the blizzard still blowing, he took the young Russian, Dimitri Gerof, and two dog teams in search of Evans and Lashly. Almost two days later, largely because of a chance break in the weather, he found them, both still alive. Much later, back in England, Crean and Lashly were presented with richly deserved medals for saving their companion's life. But Evans's sickness had consequences for which no one had planned.

According to Scott's orders, Atkinson was supposed to take the dogs south to One Ton Depot and meet the Polar Party, who in theory were only a couple of weeks behind. But Atkinson was still worried that Evans might die; as the doctor, he felt he had to stay at the Hut. I would have to go south in his stead.

A bad navigator, inexperienced with dogs, blind as a bat,

and still exhausted from over 1,000 miles of sledging, I was not the best man for the job, but I was the man available for the job. With only the young and unexperienced Dimitri for company, I set off once more onto the Barrier, thanking God that the dogs were doing the work. We made twenty miles a day and reached One Ton in only a week, on 3 March. When we arrived, however, it "blizzed" severely. Pinned down in the tent, I had several days in which to contemplate a nasty dilemma.

The Polar Party was not at One Ton. The dog food, supposedly depoted there, was missing, apparently forgotten. Should I continue south in search of the Polar Party? I could now do so only by the brutal expedient of killing the weakest dogs to feed the strongest—and Scott had given clear orders to spare the dogs for later sledging. I might have ignored that order had I known that the Polar Party was already in serious trouble, but I had no reason to think so: we had been instructed to meet them at about this date, not rescue them. Besides, my eyesight and navigation skills made it all but certain I would miss the five men unless I was actually at the depot.

I waited as long as I could, agonising about what to do, and then the dog food we had brought with us started to run out. At the same time, Dimitri suddenly fell ill with hemiplegia, a temporary but almost complete paralysis of the right side of his body. On 10 March, after making the decision to go back, I scratched a note on a small piece of paper, folded it so that it would fit into a metal canister, and tied the canister to a bamboo marker pole:

Sir,

We leave here this morning with the dogs for Hut Point. We have made no depots on the way in being off the course all the way, & so I have not been able to leave a note before.

Yours sincerely, Apsley Cherry Garrard

There followed eight days of frightening struggle. Dimitri was incoherent, possibly dying; I was terrified of getting lost in the roaring drift; the dogs were near madness with hunger. When we reached Hut Point, Dimitri was immediately added to Atch's list of patients and quickly recovered. To tell the truth, I was added to the list, too; I was exhausted and demoralised beyond anything in my experience, and desperately worried that I had done the wrong thing. Would it have been better, would it have been more the hero's role, to ignore my orders? Should I have thrown caution to the freezing wind and simply plunged on southward from One Ton, in the hope of intercepting the Polar Party? If I had done so, could two broken men and a few deranged dogs have been any help? For two weeks I did nothing but sleep, sit, churn over these questions, and start coming to terms with the growing probability that Scott, Taff, Titus, Bill, and Birdie were all dead.

Had I known that they were already in trouble. Had I learned better navigation skills. Had the depot been laid with dog food. Had I continued south just a few days more.

Then, perhaps.

I have had to learn, by slow degrees over many years, to live with two contradictory facts: that I did what made sense at the time, given what I knew at the time; and that, however irrationally, I can never quite forgive myself for not knowing and acting otherwise.

●━●━●

How grandly we had all imagined that final, triumphant photograph! Brave grins basking in the delight of victory before a fluttering Union Jack! The photograph was taken, sure enough. One can see Birdie's exposed fingers as he pulled the string, even see the string if one looks carefully. The Union Jack is there. But it was not the kind of photograph we had had in mind at all.

They reached the Pole on 17 January 1912, having passed marker flags that told them Amundsen's Norwegian expedi-

Pushing on with Scott, Birdie, and Bill: Taff Evans (left) and Titus Oates

tion had beaten them.* They had already been working for weeks at high altitude, in conditions far beyond what most men could have survived. Taff, nursing a wounded hand that would not heal, may already have had blood poisoning. Titus's thigh wound was developing from a nuisance into a dangerous problem. Birdie, Bill, and Scott were not sick, yet, not more than mildly frost-bitten, yet, but the photograph they took shows a desolation in their faces, in the way they hold themselves, in the way their eyes seem to stare beyond the camera. They knew, already, that the door through which they might return was closing.

---

*The Norwegian expedition arrived a month earlier, on 14 December. Amundsen left a letter addressed to Scott, offering him the use of equipment they had left behind and wishing him a safe return. He also left a letter to King Haakon of Norway, and a note to Scott asking that he deliver it in case Amundsen and his men did not return alive. Ironically, the British expedition's sole Norwegian, Tryggve Gran, recorded in his diary that he nearly threw this letter away by accident.

"It is a terrible disappointment, and I am very sorry for my loyal companions," Scott wrote. "All the daydreams must go; it will be a wearisome return." The next day he added: "Great God this is an awful place and terrible enough for us to have laboured to it without the reward of priority. Now for the run home and a desperate struggle to get the news through first. I wonder if we can do it."

He knew they needed luck on their side. Instead, it turned viciously against them. The weather was terrible. Taff sank into a delirium and then died on the Beardmore.* Fuel cans at the depots were half-empty from evaporation. Titus's leg worsened to the point where he could not pull and was slowing the other three down. Above all: conditions on the Barrier, instead of being better than on the Plateau, were freakishly worse.

They got a decent feed of pony meat at "slaughter camp," but by that time Titus's feet were black from frostbite and his left thigh a mass of rotting tissue. About this time he actually slit his bag open—either because it was the only way to get his bad leg in and out or because the pain was less if he kept his leg outside the bag at night and it stayed frozen. On or about 16 March, he entrusted his diary to Bill, saying, "Give this to my mother," and asked for morphine. No doubt he expected Bill to take the hint and give him a lethal overdose. Instead, all he got was a good night's sleep. When he woke up, he found

---

*He died near the foot of the glacier in the early hours of 18 February. Whether his sudden decline was due to a brain injury from an earlier fall, blood poisoning from his infected hand, or some other cause is not known.

that it was, probably, his thirty-second birthday. With an actual temperature of −40°F and a strong wind blowing, the effective temperature was about −90°F. Mumbling something about it being "time to go outside," he climbed out of the tent in his socks and crawled away to die.*

Oates died to give the remaining three a chance, but it was

Not the first: their slumping shoulders tell the whole story

---

*Scott famously recorded that Oates's last words were "I am just going outside and I may be some time." But neither Wilson nor Bowers made any note of this, and the remark makes little sense given that Oates was deliberately walking to his death. It is worth remembering that a blizzard was blowing and the noise inside the tent would have been deafening; whatever Oates did say, Scott probably could not hear it. It seems clear, also, that he did not want to hear anything that forced him to accept that Oates was committing suicide. On balance, it seems likely that Oates actually said something else. Perhaps it was "I am going outside. I think it's about time."

They knew, already, that the door through which they might return was closing: (from left) Titus, Birdie, Scott, Bill, and Taff at the Pole

too late. Bill was snow-blind and his feet frost-bitten. Scott's feet were even worse: he confided to his diary that "amputation is the best I can hope for now." Somehow they managed to drag themselves on for five more days. On 21 March, they arrived at a point just eleven miles from One Ton.* There, pegged down by a blizzard, their fuel gone, they lay in their bags and wrote farewell letters by the light of a crude lamp that they had made from a tin and some short pieces of the lampwick that Scott had been using to bind his finnesko.

It is often said that they died close to safety: not really. That they managed to keep going for five days after Titus's

---

*Nautical miles. Equal to 12½ statute, or "road," miles.

death is almost miraculous. That those five days took them only fifteen miles tells its own story. For men with a heavy sledge, ruined feet, and neither food to eat nor the means to stay warm, that same distance again might as well have been infinite. Even if they (or Bill and Birdie alone) had reached the stores at One Ton, it was another two weeks of hard travel, by the standards of fit men in good weather, to the real safety of Hut Point. That which had seemed difficult, in the planning, had become impossible.

●━━●━━●

The winter darkness began again on 23 April. It was a far deeper darkness this time. The atmosphere during the first winter had been convivial, relaxed, almost jolly. The winter of 1912, the winter of waiting, was another thing altogether.

Ponko and several others had returned to New Zealand in the *Terra Nova*, leaving a rump of just thirteen men at Cape Evans. Atch Atkinson was expedition leader in Scott's absence. He was wonderful, but his job was less like running an expedition than like being father, mother, and priest to a grieving family. There was too little to do, too much to think about. Every shadow and every sound seemed sure to be, and was not, the Polar Party returning.* Earlier, Atch had taken Keo-

---

*Here is a thing too ridiculous to be true, yet it happened. One day Tryggve Gran heard knocking above the blizzard and rushed outside. He saw a dark figure looming in the drift and ran towards it with his heart pounding. He was within arm's reach before he realised that his mind was playing tricks with the scale of things, as so often happens in the featureless Antarctic. The tall, dark visitor was a three-foot Emperor penguin.

hane on a three-day trip onto the Barrier, hoping against hope that in the crumbling light they would see something. They saw nothing, but the fact that we expected this made their news no easier to bear. We did not know it at the time but Scott, Bill, and Birdie were probably still alive when Atch and Keohane left (27 March) and dead by the time they returned (30 March).

For six months I did very little except read Charles Dickens and H. Rider Haggard, paint landscapes that looked like a dog's breakfast, and play billiards rather well on our rickety portable table. I also became the expedition's semi-official historian, because others had more or less given up their diaries while I found that writing helped me get through the day. Mostly I nursed bad headaches and stared at the walls of the hut while living in my memories. Gradually the light returned—and I hated it passionately, because some part of me clung to the idea, all evidence aside, that while it was still dark the Polar Party might return.

●━●━●

On 29 October, our Search Party moved south from Cape Evans towards the Barrier. For two weeks we skied or plodded almost in silence. My own view was that all five men had vanished forever down a crevasse. But perhaps they had simply veered off course, or died of scurvy in a drifted-over tent we would never see. In any event, there was a good chance we would find nothing; we nearly did just that.

On 7 November, Atch thought he saw a tent in the distance, but it turned out to be a trick of the light. Four days later our hearts were in our throats as we approached One Ton, every one of us hoping to find evidence that the Polar Party had reached it. Again, nothing. Then, on 12 November, it was Silas's turn to spot something, a hummock that didn't look natural, a mile or so to the right of our path. At first he ignored it and plodded on. Finally, still unsure that it was of any significance, he told everyone to stop. He skied over to it and found six inches of canvas poking out above the snow. I can still feel the thudding in my ribs as he came back and said: "It is the tent."

We dug away the accumulated drift. Atch went in first, because he was now expedition leader, taking Lashly with him, perhaps because Lashly was oldest or because it was Lashly who had seen them last. A few minutes later Lashly came out, silent, his face wet. Atch followed, carrying the neat bundle that was their letters and diaries. We listened while he read out passages from Scott's diary, describing what had happened since Taff's death. Some of that diary was to become famous,

The Search Party near Hut Point, 1 November 1912

but I went into the tent afterwards and found two pieces of paper that meant even more to me. Bill and Birdie were lying at peace in their sleeping bags. I could scarcely bring myself to look at their yellow, waxen faces. In their pockets I found three notes that

I had left for them during my own retreat down the Beardmore. They were dated "Xmas Eve," "28 Dec. lunchtime," and "29 Dec. morning." Each note wished them a safe return.

Atch asked that everyone present go in so that there would be no arguments later about exactly what we had found. Then we collapsed the tent and built a great cairn of snow over their resting place. Under a sky ablaze with iridescent cloud, we took off our hats in the frigid wind while Atch read Scott's Message to the Public, then got out a Bible and read the Burial Service. Finally someone said that "Onward, Christian Soldiers" had been Scott's favourite hymn, so we sang that as best we could, in our reedy, faltering voices.

We topped the cairn with a cross. In a metal canister attached to a pole we left a note, signed by all of us:

November 12th, 1912. Lat. 79°50'S.

This Cross and Cairn are erected over the bodies of Capt. Scott, C.V.O., R.N.; Dr. E. A. Wilson, M.B., B.A. Cantab.; Lt. H. R. Bowers, Royal Indian Marines. A slight token to perpetuate their gallant and successful attempt to reach the Pole. This they did on the 17th January 1912 after the Norwegian expedition had already done so. Inclement weather and lack of fuel was the cause of their death.

Also to commemorate their two gallant comrades, Capt. L. E. G. Oates of the Inniskilling Dragoons, who walked to his death in a blizzard to save his comrades, about 18 miles south of this position; also of Seaman Edgar Evans, who died at the foot of the Beardmore Glacier.

*The Lord gave and the Lord taketh away. Blessed be the
name of the Lord.*

Relief Expedition

We carried on for another ten miles or more south, looking for Titus's body and hoping to pay him the same respects,
but the weather made a real search impossible. We found only
his sleeping bag, a theodolite, some socks, and his finnesko.
One of the finnesko had been split open down the front, so
that he could get his frozen foot in and out of it. On another
marker pole we placed another note:

*Hereabouts died a very gallant gentleman, Captain L. E. G.
Oates of the Inniskilling Dragoons. In March 1912, returning from the Pole, he walked willingly to his death in a blizzard to try and save his comrades, beset by hardship.*

As we retreated north once more, I experienced what may
seem a foolish emotion in the circumstances. I was angry with
Antarctica. My friends had loved this great continent, and she
had returned their love by killing them. Like them, I had
dreamed of coming here and exploring in the name of science.

The dream had come true.

I never wanted to see the place again.

☙☙☙

The *Terra Nova* had spent the winter in New Zealand. We expected her back about Christmas; when she had not shown

CAPTAIN SCOTT'S TOMB NEAR THE SOUTH POLE.

The Daily Mirror

24 Pages

THE MORNING JOURNAL WITH THE SECOND LARGEST NET SALE.

No. 2,987. Registered at the G.P.O. as a Newspaper. WEDNESDAY, MAY 21, 1913 One Halfpenny.

THE MOST WONDERFUL MONUMENT IN THE WORLD: CAPTAIN SCOTT'S SEPULCHRE ERECTED AMID ANTARCTIC WASTES.

It was within a mere eleven miles of One Ton camp, which would have meant safety to the Antarctic explorers, that the search party found the tent containing the bodies of Captain Scott, Dr. E. A. Wilson and Lieutenant H. R. Bowers. This is, perhaps, the most tragic note of the whole Antarctic disaster. Above is the cairn, surmounted with a cross, erected over the tent where the bodies were found. At the side are Captain Scott's skis planted upright in a small pile of frozen snow.—(Copyright in England. Droits de reproduction en France reservées.)

up by mid-January, we started to contemplate what we would have to do to survive another winter in Antarctica. But on 18 January she finally arrived—she had, again, been stuck for weeks in terrible pack ice.

All her flags were flying; champagne and cigars had been laid out in celebration. They did not know, of course.

"Are you all well?" the captain shouted through a tin megaphone. There was a long pause before anyone could summon up the courage to tell the news: "The Polar Party died on their return from the Pole. We have their records." The flags came down. The champagne was put away unopened.

The *Terra Nova*'s carpenter built a beautiful wooden cross out of jarrah, an extremely hard and durable species of eucalyptus. It was so heavy that I and seven other men were needed to drag it 750 feet up Observation Hill, above Hut Point. We had considered various Bible verses as an inscription. In the end I was glad that, at my suggestion, we used instead the last line of "Ulysses," Tennyson's great hymn to the heroic spirit: "To strive, to seek, to find, and not to yield."

The cross faces south, across the Barrier.

"A grave which kings must envy": More than a year after his death, Scott's final resting place makes the newspapers. The Daily Mirror *was wrong about Scott's ski, however; Gran's ski were used to make the cross, and Gran then skied back to Cape Evans on Scott's pair, so that they at least would return*

9

"WHAT IS THE USE?"

THE BERKELEY HOTEL,
LONDON, MAY 1959

I AM SITTING in a high-backed wicker chair, at a breakfast table in an old hotel. Angela, my wife, has just tucked a
tartan blanket around my legs. Perhaps she saw my hands
shaking and thought I was cold. Or perhaps she wanted to
think I was cold, because then she would not have to think
that I am old, sick, and dying. In front of me, on the table, are
the remains of my breakfast. A pot of tea. Some buttered toast.
A half-finished bowl of tinned peaches in syrup.

*Roald Amundsen
in his furs*

People like to compare Amundsen and Scott, arguing about
who was the better explorer or the greater man. I need to say
something about that.

Amundsen was superb. He planned brilliantly, knew the
value of expert dog-handling, and took men who could ski
before they could walk. He was a great leader, too, at least
by some accounts: calm, decisive, good at making his men

Oscar Wisting with the Norwegian flag at the South Pole, December 1911

work well together. Finally, he was immensely lucky, and although he disliked taking risks, he chose his risks well. He cut a hundred miles from the Polar journey by camping directly on the Barrier, which might have broken off at any time. Heading south, he found by pure chance an unknown glacier that was closer to the Pole than the Beardmore (thus cutting down his time on the high Plateau) and much easier to climb because it had fewer crevasses. The lowest temperature on his entire journey was −24°F. Because of all these things, he took the Pole as one might take a strenuous walk after lunch. He took it as if he felt that, for the right man with the right equipment, it was a thoroughly enjoyable way to get some light exercise in the sunshine.

Well, I exaggerate. He had hard work, some nasty disagreements with his men, and some rough days. He also made small, comical mistakes, like forgetting to bring a snow shovel to Antarctica, and large, not so comical mistakes, like setting out for the Pole too early in September and wasting a week being beaten back to camp by a blizzard. But it was easy, in the end: he said as much himself. The same journey turned into

an epic of lethal horror for Taff, Titus, Scott, Birdie, and Bill—
five of the toughest men who have ever drawn breath. Why the
difference?

I would be lying if I said that I do not blame Scott to some
degree. He could be impulsive. He was capable of planning
poorly, not sharing his plans, and shredding his plans with
last-minute decisions that made no sense. He could be a difficult man, too, cheery one day and peevish the next. And he
was stubborn. Knowing little about dogs, he had a bad time
with them on the *Discovery* expedition, but his response, instead of trying to learn more, was to blame the dogs and rely
next time on ponies, which he chose without sufficient care.
(Titus recognised at once that our Manchurian steeds were
poor material. He got small thanks for breaking the news.)

All of this and much more has been said in criticism of
Scott. All of it will be said again, because the world is full of
little men who just can't make the distance from breakfast to
lunch without mocking their betters. Very few of the most
popular criticisms stick, actually: the great majority of the
"mistakes" of which Scott has been accused from time to time
were not mistakes at all. He was wrong to rely on ponies and
man-haulage so much and on dogs so little—but in fact he had
excellent reasons for his choice.* He gave muddled orders

---

*With more dogs, and better-trained dog drivers, Scott could have crossed the
Barrier earlier and faster, as Amundsen did. At the time, though, he had two
good reasons for not relying heavily on them. First, he suspected that they would
be useless in the huge pressure ridges of the Beardmore Glacier. Second, his best
source of information on travelling the Barrier, outside his own experience, was
Shackleton—and it was Shackleton who, having read about the use of ponies in
Siberia and Manchuria, first proposed taking them to Antarctica. Shackleton
wrote enthusiastically about them after the *Nimrod* expedition, claiming they

about what to do with the dog teams—but in fact his orders were both sensible and prudently flexible. He should have used Inuit-style fur clothing instead of windproof cotton—but, as anyone knows who has actually hauled a sledge, this is nonsense. He should have insisted that sledge teams take cocoa rather than the nutritionally empty tea—but in fact he had engaged in open discussion (and had clear reasons for his preference) on even this minute point.

Anyway, even the sound points miss the point. Robert Falcon Scott was a giant, a man of irresistible vision, energy, enterprise, and charm. He was not a bad leader, or a good leader; he was an exceptionally great one. His keen insight led him to pick men who got along with one another. His genuine interest in every problem and activity made everyone feel valued: if he had finished quizzing Silas Wright about abstruse geomagnetic experiments, or chiding the biologists for not being clear about what they meant by the term *degenerate form*, he would turn around and start a conversation with Trigger Gran about Norwegian literature or politics. The reserved and brittle man of myth was actually exactly the opposite. If you read the diaries and letters of his men, even the private writings into which people naturally spill their irritation or anger, what you find for the most part is loyalty based on admiration. Teddy

Not a bad leader, or a good leader; he was an exceptionally great one—and very hard to keep up with on ski: Captain Robert Falcon Scott

---

were more efficient over ice than dogs. Scott's own experiences, while setting up a base camp and laying depots in the summer and autumn of 1911, tended to confirm this: he was "astonished at the strength" of the ponies, and at the same time he noted that the dogs "are getting better, but they only take very light loads still and get back from each journey pretty dead beat."

Evans was one of the few members of the expedition with whom Scott truly had a hard time getting along. Yet he summed up the general attitude to Scott in two words: "fanatical devotion."

Certainly Scott's mental and physical stamina were not matched by anyone, even on this expedition, not even by titans like Bill, Birdie, William Lashly, and Tom Crean. Because of luck, the simplicity of his aims, and (mostly) good planning, Amundsen never had to endure a hundredth part of what Scott's Polar Party endured. Despite terrible luck, hugely more ambitious aims, and admittedly some poor planning, they completed nine-tenths of a journey so brutally severe and so epic in scope that it will never be equaled, in Antarctica or anywhere else. Not one man in ten thousand could have done what Scott did. And not one in a million could have ended it as Scott did, composing some of the most generous and most heartbreakingly beautiful lines ever penned as he lay in that tent, crippled by frostbite and dying of starvation and cold.*

❦❦❦

As for Bill and Birdie: nearly fifty years have passed and yet they are with me constantly. Sometimes I think of them laughing and joking around the cooker after a good day's sledging. Sometimes I think of them lying on either side of Scott: three stone effigies, taking their eternal rest in a green canvas church that no parishioner visits.

*See Chapter 10, "Last Words."

They did not live to see the Great War, or the greater war that followed. They were not there to share my sadness on reading in *The Times*, in 1943, that the *Terra Nova* had sunk off Greenland.* They did not survive to witness the destruction of the world they knew. Some comfort there. Sometimes I would give back all the extra years, the years they were denied, in order to be with them.

In February 1913, the *Terra Nova* had carried us back to New Zealand—another rough go, in which we were nearly crushed by icebergs before facing more storms. In March I took a steamer back to England. I had picked the husky Krisravitza, Birdie's special favourite, to take home with me. Her name supposedly means "most beautiful" in Russian, though "most lazy" was closer to the mark. I hoped that she would find retirement at an English country house some compensation for her hardships; she did.

I also took home with me a small wooden box lined with straw. It contained three Emperor penguin eggs. One sunny

---

*She had returned to the Newfoundland seal fishery, but by 1943 she was being used to supply U.S. bases in Greenland. On 12 September, she left the little settlement at Julianehåb, on the western side of Greenland's southern tip, bound for St. John's. Late that evening she sprang yet another leak, and once again, her pumps failed her. By the afternoon of 13 September, when the United States Coast Guard cutter *Atak* reached her position, she was close to sinking. Conditions were so bad that it took four hours to rescue the twenty men on board; later, all four of the men who had volunteered to man the *Atak*'s lifeboat received Coast Guard medals for bravery. There was one final indignity: the captain of the *Atak* thought a half-submerged and unmanned ship would be a danger, so he used the cutter's gun to finish her off. She lies in seventy fathoms at 60°15'15" North, 45°55'45" West.

Krisravitza

day in July 1913, I took that box to the British Museum's Natural History Department. I ended up in rather a temper with one of the staff, who seemed preoccupied and would not give me so much as a receipt at first. In his defence, it was one of many visits I had made to that great terra-cotta palace of science, to deliver and discuss thousands of *Terra Nova* specimens. This man had no reason to share my feeling that these particular items were of any exalted significance. What were they, after all?

Three eggshells with rough holes cut into them; some glutinous chunks of yolk in a stoppered bottle of alcohol; another bottle containing three pickled embryos, ghostly white morsels barely three inches long that, with their huge eyes and tiny necks, looked more like insects than birds. I was aware, as this functionary could not be, of the enormous tide of effort and suffering that had borne these strange relics to the museum. I had the sense, as he did not, that in coming to the museum that day I was at long last completing the Cape Crozier journey.

That morning I was blinded by memories. The eggs simply mattered too much to me: I could not see that I was being overwrought, oversensitive, and unreasonable. So I seethed, and met rudeness with rudeness, and when that didn't work, I contemplated quite seriously the value of screaming, or saying something like "Do you have any idea what you are dealing with? Do you not understand that better men than you risked their lives to bring you these materials?" In the end, though, I allowed my knuckles to whiten in silence and I walked away. Kicking a stone along the pavement on the way back to the railway station, I comforted myself with the thought that it was Bill and Birdie who had suffered an insult, if anyone had, and that Bill and Birdie would have responded to the whole incident with gales of laughter.

Well! As it turned out, the custodian was perfectly right not to get excited. Those sad specimens lay unexamined for years, despite my sending a postcard from time to time to nudge the museum into doing something. Eventually they found their way to the right people, and as I made a point to keep up with the scientific news, I learned the worst soon enough: the eggs we so nearly died to collect were worthless. The final, politely damning word came in the journal *Zoology*, after eminent men had applied their microscopes to dozens of slides from both the Cape Crozier eggs and a series of our Adélie specimens: "It must be stated that neither has added greatly to our knowledge of penguin embryology."

Laugh, if you like. The conclusion is not entirely surprising. We dragged elaborate preserving equipment to Cape Crozier, planning to set up shop there for weeks while we pickled eggs and minutely examined them. Instead, our three pitiful eggs froze solid while we fought for our lives. Then, when we got back to Cape Evans, Bill extracted the embryos and found that they were older, and closer to hatching, than he had predicted or hoped. But the two real blows, I am happy to say, came too late for him.

First of all: Ernst Haeckel was at the height of his influence from 1900 to 1910, but by 1920 his theory was falling out of favour. He says that the features of *mature ancestors* show up in *juvenile* modern creatures. True, sometimes—but it's equally true that *mature* modern creatures sometimes resemble the *juvenile* stages of their ancestors. In neither case do we really understand why, and in both cases biologists have concluded that the phenomenon reveals little about the animal's evolutionary history.

Second: it turns out that penguins are not "primitive" birds at all. In 1903, Bill made an educated guess that they evolved directly from flightless ancestors—that they were, so to speak, halfway between the dinosaur and the albatross. On the contrary. Modern ornithologists think that the ancestors of penguins flew just as well as other birds. The reason penguins don't fly is that Antarctica became a cold place, where losing the ability to fly was a fair exchange for becoming fat and good at swimming. Any similarity between penguins and "primitive flightless birds" is coincidence.

These developments are what you come to expect from good science. There will always be ten blind alleys for each advance, and each blind alley demands to be explored. Alas, what you must also come to expect is that the discovery of a blind alley only confirms the most cynical suspicions of the armchair men, who have never explored anything and who make themselves feel better by sniggering that our kind of business was a waste of effort. "What is the use? What is the point? Why did you bother?" That is their mantra. Poor devils! The armchair men who speak of wasted effort cannot bear the other possibility: that you waste a life by choosing comfort over knowledge, that you waste a life by taking no risks, that

you waste a life by combining fear of the unknown with complacency about everything else.

A painting by Bill of Cape Evans in winter

Bill Wilson was too good a scientist and too good a man to have either of these faults. And he was spot-on about one thing. Teeth or no, the birds did evolve from the dinosaurs.

●━●━●

Those two terrible, gruelling years in the South, with all their physical and mental suffering, were the best in my long life; I would not give them up (as Birdie would have put it) for all the tea in China. I learned how to live down there. I learned how wonderful it is to be freed from caring about all the little things in life that obsess us, peck away at us, and don't matter. Above all: I got to see the pure shining gold that is in some men.

For a man not to fear death is remarkable. But for men to respond to unrelenting physical pain and terrifying danger by always thinking of others before themselves; for men to be capable of making light-hearted jokes out of the most crushing disappointments; for men to find within themselves, at the worst of times, the spirit of the cheerful optimist—I would exchange a hundred years of armchairs for the privilege of having seen that such things are possible.

Here's something you may find it hard to believe, but I believe it: Bill did not care that Amundsen beat them to the Pole. The disappointment would have broken some men, because some men think that life is a competition. Scott suffered, though even he was in two minds about the value of going there: his diaries show that making the expedition useful was always more important to him than beating Amundsen. Bill Wilson was a different sort of creature entirely, that rare man who does not think about himself at all. As a young student he had scribbled in a notebook: "This is the most fascinating ideal I think I ever imagined, to become entirely careless of your own soul and body in looking after the welfare of others." Unlike many earnest young men who dream of becoming something special, Bill lived that ideal. He went to the Pole for the same reason he went to Cape Crozier: because the world is a beautiful, wonderful place and he felt compelled to experience, understand, and share it. I hesitate to describe him as selfless, though, because that might suggest he was saintly, and therefore boring. He *was* selfless, and a saint, too. But perhaps you would need to have seen him leaping about the decks of the *Terra Nova*, stark naked, laughing and throwing buckets of water at people, to understand what I mean.

Bill and Birdie set the highest standard I have known for what it is to be human, and their inspiration lives on. I receive letters from around the world, written by ordinary men and women facing pain, disease, grief. They all say the same thing: "Knowing the story you tell of these men and how they held on to hope when all hope was gone and faced death itself with such quiet courage, has given me strength." That is Bill and Birdie's monument. It is taller and more beautiful than the pyramids.

When I had come out of that silent tent on the Barrier and was on my knees in the snow, sobbing without restraint, Tryggve Gran came over and put his arm around me. "Cherry," he said after a while, "the important thing is that they died having done something great. They are happy now. Just think how much harder death must be, for men who have done nothing!"

Gran was right. But he was thinking of the Pole, and that was not their great achievement. On their sledge, to the very end, they pulled thirty-five pounds of extraordinary rocks that they had collected during their return down the Beardmore. "Fools," the armchair men all say. "They should have dumped them." No, as a matter of fact: Bill insisted that they keep them all, and he was right. Those precious stones included Jurassic dolerites, fragments from a thick seam of coal, and the first fossils proving that long ago the fern *Glossopteris* waved its

fronds over warm Antarctic soil. If they had dumped those rocks, which transformed our understanding of a continent, they would probably have died anyway. In either case, they would have sledged and suffered in vain. But it's no use talking to some people about the idea of loving knowledge more than your own life.*

●━●━●

Over the years I have spent many a July afternoon, armed with my notebook and binoculars, on birding walks over the English countryside. As I watch a pair of linnets or yellowhammers frolic in the soft summer air, I think of their flightless cousins the Emperors, huddling together once more at the bottom of the world to protect their eggs from the murderous cold of another Cape Crozier winter.

Emperor of the Ice: Aptenodytes forsteri

They were standing on that fringe of ice a thousand winters before we ever saw them. They will be standing there still, a thousand winters after you and I are dust. I have always found something deeply moving in their absolute, inhuman tenacity. And sometimes it strikes me that Birdie, with his big chest and hooked nose and short legs, looked a bit like an Emperor penguin. Perhaps that was his secret.

---

* *Glossopteris* proved especially important. The pattern of its worldwide distribution became a clue to the reality of Alfred Wegener's much-mocked theory that the continents drift.

10

LAST WORDS

THESE LETTERS AND NOTES were all written either at the last camp or very near it during the week or ten days leading up to 29 March 1912.

From Scott's letter to his friend Sir J. M. Barrie, creator of Peter Pan:

The cross on Observation Hill

> *We are in a desperate state, feet frozen, etc. No fuel and a long way from food, but it would do your heart good to be in our tent, to hear our songs and the cheery conversation as to what we will do when we get to Hut Point.*
>
> *[Later:] We are very near the end, but have not and will not lose our good cheer. We have had four days of storm in our tent and nowhere's food or fuel. I never met a man in my life whom I admired and loved more than you, but I never could show you how much your friendship meant to me, for you had so much to give and I nothing.*

From Scott's letter to his wife, Kathleen:

Dear it is not easy to write because of the cold—70 degrees below zero and nothing but the shelter of our tent—you know I have loved you, you know my thoughts must have constantly dwelt on you and oh dear me you must know that quite the worst aspect of this situation is the thought that I shall not see you again— The inevitable must be faced . . .

Since writing the above we have got to within 11 miles of our depot with one hot meal and two days' cold food and we should have got through but have been held for four days by a frightful storm—I think the best chance has gone. We have decided not to kill ourselves but to fight it to the last for that depot but in the fighting there is a painless end so don't worry.

What lots and lots I could tell you of this journey. How much better it has been than lounging in comfort at home. What tales you would have for the boy*—but oh what a price to pay—to forfeit the sight of your dear dear face.

From Scott's letter to Mrs. Emily Bowers:

I am afraid that this will reach you after one of the heaviest blows of your life. I write when we are very near the end of our journey, and I am finishing it in the company of two

---

*Their son, Peter Markham Scott, was two years old in 1912. In the same letter, Scott also wrote, "Make the boy interested in natural history if you can, it is better than games." Apparently she did: he grew up to become a world-renowned ornithologist and conservationist.

gallant, noble gentlemen. One of these is your son. He has come to be one of my closest and soundest friends, and I appreciate his wonderful upright nature, his ability and energy. As the troubles have thickened his dauntless spirit ever shone brighter and he has remained cheerful, hopeful and indomitable to the end.

From Scott's letter to Oriana Wilson, Bill's wife:

If this letter reaches you, Bill and I will have gone out together. We are very near it now and I would like you to know how splendid he was at the end—everlastingly cheerful and ready to sacrifice himself for others, never a word of blame to me for leading him into this mess. I can do no more to comfort you than to tell you that he died as he lived, a brave, true man—the best of comrades and staunchest of friends. My whole heart goes out to you in pity.

From Wilson's letter to his wife, Oriana:

God be with you in your troubles dear, when I am gone—my love is as living for you as ever . . . We have struggled to the end and we have nothing to regret . . . Two of the five of us are dead. The rest of us are fit to go on, only God seems to wish otherwise as he has given us quite impossible weather and we are now clean run out of food and fuel . . . It is God's will and all is for the best. I have had a very happy life and look forward to a very happy life hereafter when we shall all be together again. Your little testament and prayer book will be in my hand or in my pocket when the end comes. All is well.

From Bowers's letter to his mother:

When man's extremity is reached God's help may see things right & tho' the end will be painless enough for myself, I should so like to come through for your dear sake. It is splendid however to pass with such companions as I have & as all 5 of us have mothers and 3 wives you will not be alone. Your ever loving son to the end of this life & the next where God shall wipe away all tears from our eyes.

From Scott's Message to the Public:

Had we but lived, I would have had a tale to tell of the hardihood, endurance and courage of my companions which would have stirred the heart of every Englishman. These rough notes and our dead bodies must tell the tale.

From Scott's diary:

Last Entry. For God's sake look after our people.

CHRONOLOGY

A SCURVY NOTE

THANKS

SOURCES

CHRONOLOGY

(1901–04)

Robert Falcon Scott goes to Antarctica for the first time, aboard the *Discovery*. Bill Wilson is Assistant Surgeon.

November 1902: Scott's "farthest south" with Wilson and Ernest Shackleton, less than 500 miles from the South Pole.

September and October 1903: Wilson and others make two sledge journeys from Hut Point to Cape Crozier.

(1906)

Roald Amundsen, aboard the *Gjøa*, becomes the first man to navigate the Northwest Passage from the Atlantic to the Pacific.

(1907–09)

Shackleton's *Nimrod* expedition.

January 1909: Shackleton reaches the Polar Plateau by climbing the Beardmore Glacier and records a new "farthest south," less than 100 miles from the South Pole.

September 1909: The Americans Robert Peary and Frederick Cook both claim priority in reaching the North Pole.* Scott announces his new British Antarctic Expedition.

(1910)

15 June: The *Terra Nova* leaves Cardiff for New Zealand.

29 November: The *Terra Nova* leaves New Zealand for Antarctica.

(1911)

4 January: The *Terra Nova* arrives at Cape Evans. Sledge teams spend the autumn laying supply depots for the coming year.

23 April: Last of the sun: the first winter begins.

22 June: The Midwinter Day dinner.

27 June–1 August: The Winter Journey to Cape Crozier and back.

22 August: Return of the sun.

1 November: Pony teams leave Cape Evans on the Polar Journey.

---

*Peary's claim persuaded Amundsen, who had been planning a North Pole expedition, to turn south. Ironically, Cook's claim to have reached the North Pole was almost certainly fraudulent, and Peary's remains doubtful. In the end, Amundsen did become the first person (along with his companions, Lincoln Ellsworth and Umberto Nobile) with an indisputable claim to have seen the North Pole; they overflew it, in 1926, in the airship *Norge*.

14 December: Amundsen reaches the South Pole with Oscar Wisting, Olav Bjaaland, Sverre Hassel, and Helmer Hanssen.

21 December: First Returning Party turns back near the top of the Beardmore Glacier.

(1912)

4 January: Second Returning Party turns back from the Polar Plateau.

17 January: Polar Party reaches the South Pole.

22 January: The *Terra Nova* returns from New Zealand with supplies and mail. Archer and Williamson join the Shore Party while nine of the existing Shore Party—including Taylor, Ponting, and Clissold—return to New Zealand. This leaves thirteen men at Cape Evans for the second winter.

18 February: Taff Evans dies on the lower Beardmore.

7 March: Amundsen's expedition, in the *Fram*, reaches Tasmania.

16 or 17 March: Titus Oates dies on the Barrier.

29 March (approximately): Wilson, Bowers, and Scott die on the Barrier near One Ton Depot.

23 April: Last of the sun: the second winter begins.

29 October: The Search Party leaves Cape Evans.

12 November: Silas Wright finds Scott's tent.

(1913)

18 January: The *Terra Nova*, with the recovered Teddy Evans on board, arrives in McMurdo Sound and picks up the survivors.

10 February: The *Terra Nova* reaches New Zealand.

March: Cherry returns to England on the steamer *Osterley*.

14 June: The *Terra Nova* returns to Cardiff, a day short of three years after leaving.

14 July: Probable date of Cherry's visit to deliver the Cape Crozier eggs to the Natural History Museum.

(1922)

4 December: *The Worst Journey in the World* is published by Constable and Company in London.

(1939)

6 September: Cherry marries Angela Turner.

(1943)

13 September: The *Terra Nova* sinks off Greenland.

(1959)

18 May: Cherry dies in London; he is buried alongside his ancestors at St. Helen's, Wheathampstead, two miles from the family home at Lamer.

Many of Scott's men exchanged the horrors of Antarctica for the horrors of war. Cherry served only briefly, in the new Royal Naval Air Service; he was quickly sidelined by a physical collapse brought on by his Antarctic experiences and was a semi-invalid for the rest of his life. Atch Atkinson survived both Gallipoli and the battle of the Somme, and won several medals for bravery; Victor Campbell and Teddy Evans were also decorated for bravery. Frank Debenham, William Lashly, Silas Wright, and Anton Omelchenko also saw action, and Tryggve Gran, who joined the Royal Flying Corps, became an air ace and shot down seventeen German planes. In 1928, when Amundsen disappeared near the North Pole, Gran was part of the search; he was also the longest-surviving officer of the expedition, dying in Norway in 1980.

Tom Crean enlisted to fight in the war, but got a second dose of Antarctic horror instead when the Navy assigned him to Shackleton's ill-fated *Endurance* expedition. His service for Shackleton was characterized by the usual combination of self-effacement and jaw-dropping heroism—but that is another story. In 1920 he retired to the place of his birth, the Dingle Peninsula in County Kerry, and opened a pub. It still stands, and still bears the name he gave it: The South Pole Inn.

A SCURVY NOTE

Scurvy is a horrible way to go. Your gums swell and bleed, your skin goes pale, and you bruise very easily. You are exhausted. Then your teeth come loose and your hair falls out. Stiffness and pain start, often in the backs of the legs. Wounds fail to heal. Old wounds break open and start to rot.

Between about 1600 and 1800, tens of thousands of sailors were sewn into their hammocks and dumped into the sea after dying this way. Then, in 1747, the Scottish physician James Lind introduced citrus fruits into the Royal Navy diet. Scurvy deaths among sailors declined steeply—and some people think that is the end of the story. So it isn't surprising that a myth has got about: the causes of the disease were well understood by 1910—and if Scott's men died of it, he must have been guilty of negligence.

The truth is very different. In 1910 a now largely forgotten debate still raged. Scott, just like the great Norwegian explorer Fridtjof Nansen, got his opinions on the disease from people who had turned decisively *away* from the idea that citrus juices were a cure-all.

Edward Atkinson, Scott's medical man, was typical: he had seen considerable evidence against the "juice theory" and favoured instead the view that scurvy was probably a form of blood poisoning caused by spoiled food. Far from ignoring the disease, he continually monitored the men's blood acidity to detect such poisoning. He was not narrow-minded, though: he knew perfectly well that fresh fruits and vegetables, and also fresh meat, sometimes helped prevent scurvy. But it was unclear in 1910–12 how much value these foods had as a cure (because of a special substance they contained), as opposed to how useful they were as a preventative (because of contaminants they lacked). The real route to prevention, Atkinson believed, was a diet of fresh *and therefore uncontaminated* food. Atkinson suspected that citrus juices were useful, if at all, only because their acidity killed off the bacteria that caused the blood poisoning.

Scott and Atkinson could not have known why the "juice theory" had come under doubt again in the Navy. We do now. Scurvy is a deficiency of ascorbic acid (vitamin C). If your diet contains none, you remain healthy for at most a few months. Scurvy decreased in the Navy when the juice of Mediterranean *lemons* became a standard ration; it then increased sharply again after an apparently harmless switch to West Indian *limes*. The limes were easier to get. They also contained about two-thirds less vitamin C.

Scott's Polar Party ate both tinned beef pemmican and some fresh pony meat. Unfortunately, even fresh meat is only a modest source of vitamin C, and drying and cooking tends to destroy what little of the vitamin there is. Still, the balance of probabilities is that they did not yet have symptoms: Wilson never mentioned them, and Atkinson, who examined the bodies in the tent, found none. What killed them was probably just exhaustion, hunger, and cold.

You can read a more detailed version of this note at richardfarr.net/scurvy.html.

THANKS

They say it takes a village to raise a child. It takes a village to write a book, too, but it's a bit embarrassing to recognize that I wrote this one with the help of about as many people as Captain Scott took ashore at Cape Evans.

At the Scott Polar Research Institute in Cambridge, I got to enjoy that quintessential experience of Polar research: four o'clock tea breaks, announced by the tolling of the brass bell on the staircase: the bell of the *Terra Nova*. Equally memorable, but more unnerving, was drinking the tea next to a glass case containing Titus Oates's ripped sleeping bag—and then going back to my desk in the archive and holding in my hands the very notes that Cherry had left at cairns on the Beardmore and found again in Bill's and Birdie's pockets. Thanks to Naomi Boneham, Heather Lane, Shirley Sawtell, and Lucy Martin for making my time at SPRI efficient and productive.

At the Natural History Museum archives in London, in that lovely sanctuary hidden away behind *Diplodocus* and the café, Lesley Price did exceptionally thorough research that saved me hours and uncovered gems. Joy Wheeler, at the Royal Geographical Society, helped me with polite efficiency despite the fact that I had just got off a night flight from Seattle and kept walking into things.

The highlight of my research was a too-brief visit to the Natural History Museum Bird Group, in Tring, Hertfordshire, where Douglas Russell and Dr. Jo Cooper actually showed me those three magical eggs, the one remaining Emperor embryo, and a couple of sooty albatross that Cherry himself caught and stuffed off Tasmania. Cherry's own tiny handwritten labels are attached to the birds—"Phoebetra palabrata. Lat 44°30'S 155°E, 21st Oct '10 between NZ & Tasmania"—and, a hundred years on, they still smell of fish oil and the Southern Ocean.

Back in Seattle, Dr. Michael Toubbeh of Group Health Cooperative straightened me out, in more ways than one, and Jeremy Higgins, of the Pacific Science Center's Willard Smith Planetarium, turned me upside down and pointed me in the right direction. I received other research or technical help from Lisa Adamo (National Archives and Records Administration, Washington, D.C.), Professor Jaakko Putkonen (Department of Earth and Space Science, University of Washington), Adrian Fox (British Antarctic Survey), Scott Price (U.S. Coast Guard), Dr. Rick Roth (Department of Geography, University of Washington), and Dr. Beth Sanderson (National Oceanic and Atmospheric Administration). I also (thank goodness) submitted drafts of the manuscript to the red pens of Dr. David Amory, Douglas Russell (see above), Helen Thayer, Louise Townsend, and Jim Wickwire.

Special thanks also to my editor, Wesley Adams, his assistant, Lisa Graff, and superb copy editors Susan Brown and Karla Reganold for combining enthusiasm with fanatical attention to detail; to Leesa Brown (Seattle University), for being my expert pilot in foggy bureaucratic seas; to Edward and Sarah Bruce-White, for hospitality to uninvited literary detectives; to Sir Ranulph Fiennes, for finding the time to write to me under uniquely taxing circumstances; to my sister, Clarissa Goodbody, for lending me both her finely tuned literary ear and her finely tuned car; to John and Adam Goodbody, for essential research legwork; to Diane and Dale Ramerman, for operating the best writer's retreat in the Pacific Northwest; to my agent, Kendra Marcus, for getting the manuscript airborne; to my sons, Aidan and Declan, for the good grace with which they endured endless dinnertime twittering about matters Antarctic; and to Cherry's biographer, Sara Wheeler (see Sources), for answering numerous questions and for encouragements.

My greatest debt by far is to my wife, Kerry Fitz-Gerald. If you are ever tempted by the glamorous life of the starving writer, let me say this: you, too, should marry someone with a steady job, superb research skills, a passion for cooking, and the patience of a saint.

I have tried hard to get the facts right, but no doubt there are errors and omissions. Fortunately for me, several of the people who were kind enough to read and comment on the manuscript know far more about Antarctica than I do. They know who they are, and the story I'll be sticking to, loudly if necessary, is that any remaining imperfections are somehow their fault.

SOURCES

SHORT LIST

Antarctic literature is a vast and ever-flowing glacier. In addition to Cherry's great berg *The Worst Journey in the World*, and the writings of Scott, Wilson, and many other expedition members, I have perhaps gained most from travel writer Sara Wheeler's beautiful, elegiac biography, *Cherry*, and polar scientist Dr. Susan Solomon's analytical and persuasive postmortem, *The Coldest March*. These two authors make me wonder: What would an Edwardian traditionalist like Cherry have made of a future in which some of Antarctica's best scientists, bravest travellers, and most talented writers are women? I imagine him sitting down heavily at the big table in the hut at Cape Evans, nursing a large mug of tea, and taking half an hour to digest the idea. But not longer. Cherry was a connoisseur of good writing and even more a connoisseur of good character, especially when it showed up in slightly maverick individualists. He reserved his deepest respect for such people.

The published literature on Scott's expedition is huge—my excuses for adding to it are in the preface—but many details in this book come from unpublished diaries and papers. The resources of the library at the Natural History Museum, and especially of the archive at the Scott Polar Research Institute in Cambridge, were essential. The short list below offers brief notes on the handful of books (and films) that were most important to me. A complete bibliography follows.

Bainbridge, Beryl. *The Birthday Boys.*

A novel in five chapters. Each chapter is written in the voice of one of the five men in the Polar Party who died. See my comments in the preface.

Cherry-Garrard, Apsley. *The Worst Journey in the World.*

There are many editions available in paperback, only one of which is listed in the bibliography. They lack Wilson's drawings and paintings, which graced the original, but at least they are easy to find. You can also find the entire text—with all those illustrations—online at Project Gutenberg, www.guten berg.org. Since I'm a bit of a skeptic about the charms and wonders of computers, I should record how marvelous this is, and how helpful it was to be able to search Cherry's text electronically.

Fiennes, Sir Ranulph. *Race to the Pole: Tragedy, Heroism, and Scott's Antarctic Quest.* Published in the United Kingdom as *Captain Scott.*

A must-read. This meticulously researched book seeks to defend Scott against his critics, and in fact to undermine an entire mythology about his allegedly bad leadership, bad decision-making, and incompetence. Its memorable dedication reads: "To the families of the defamed dead." The main target of this sharp barb is Roland Huntford—see his entry.

Frend, Charles (director). *Scott of the Antarctic.*

Over sixty years old, this famous film has held up well. Despite a certain earnestness, it is well-acted and above all *accurate*; it gets the details right and manages to avoid both idolizing Scott and blaming him for everything.

Huntford, Roland. *Scott and Amundsen.* Republished as *The Last Place on Earth.*

Huntford is a beguilingly good writer, and this vicious attack on the legend of Scott's heroism has led a whole generation of people who don't know anything about it to swallow a new legend in which Scott was a bungling fool. On the Web, in particular, discussion of Scott is dominated by two sets of people: those who have found Huntford persuasive and those who have merely listened to those who have found Huntford persuasive. Don't even read Huntford—or any website that mentions Scott—unless you also read Fiennes (see his entry).

Ponting, Herbert George. *90° South.*

This film is a gem, not only because it shows you the men and the scenery as they were, in footage of astonishing quality given when and where it was shot, but because the introduction (by Ponting and Teddy Evans) reminds you how differently from modern English people they spoke. Ponting's commentary is also a refreshing reminder that it was an article of faith for these men—unlike many of their later fans and critics—not to take themselves seriously.

Scott, Robert Falcon. *Journals.*

It's not only the famous last words that glow. Scott left school just after his thirteenth birthday, to become a Naval cadet. Yet he wrote with precision, eloquence, and flair about everything he saw and everyone he met. The excellent one-volume edition edited by Max Jones has the original text plus notes on how Scott's words were sanitized for public consumption.

Solomon, Susan. *The Coldest March: Scott's Fatal Antarctic Expedition.*

One of the best books on exactly what went wrong, by a Polar scientist who is famous in her own right, both for climate studies in Antarctica and for her work on the Intergovernmental Panel on Climate Change.

Sturridge, Charles (director). *Shackleton.*

This made-for-TV movie stars Kenneth Branagh as Scott's colleague and rival. A great story lovingly re-created—and with Tom Crean at the forefront, again. But it's also worth seeing because of the huge effort its researchers and designers put into accurately depicting the clothes, boats, tents, and other equipment used. For most of us, luckily, it's the closest we'll ever come to being forced to eat our dogs while stranded on an ice cube.

Taylor, Thomas Griffith. *With Scott: The Silver Lining.*

Alas, long out of print, this is one of the best of many books by members of the *Terra Nova* expedition. Cherry makes it clear that he admired "Griff" immensely for his energy, learning, insatiable curiosity, and sense of humour; the book is full of that spirit. As Cherry put it dryly: "His gear took up more room than was strictly his share, and his mind also filled up a considerable amount of space."

Wheeler, Sara. *Cherry: A Life of Apsley Cherry-Garrard.*
An excellent biography, exquisitely written. It probably tells us everything we will ever know about Cherry but never loses sight of the fact that ultimately every life is a mystery.

Wilson, Edward Adrian. *Diary of the "Terra Nova" Expedition to the Antarctic, 1910–1912; An Account of Scott's Last Expedition.*
Wilson's diaries are a fascinating contrast with Scott's: while Scott's personality bubbles out of every paragraph, Wilson is the cool, self-effacing observer. Facts, facts, facts. As a result, his diaries are not a great read—but they are a monument to how much can be noticed when you equip a scientist with the eyes of an artist.

BIBLIOGRAPHY

Alexander, Caroline. *The Endurance: Shackleton's Legendary Antarctic Expedition.* New York: Alfred A. Knopf, 1998.

Amundsen, Roald. *Roald Amundsen: My Life as an Explorer.* Garden City, N.Y.: Doubleday, Page & Co., 1927.

———. *First Crossing of the Polar Sea.* Garden City, N.Y.: Doubleday, Doran, 1928.

———. *The South Pole: An Account of the Norwegian Antarctic Expedition in the Fram, 1910–1912.* New York: Cooper Square Press, 2001.

Aughton, Peter. *Resolution: Captain Cook's Second Voyage of Discovery.* New York: Cold Spring Press, 2005.

Bainbridge, Beryl. *The Birthday Boys.* New York: Carroll & Graf, 1994.

Bixby, William. *Robert Scott, Antarctic Pioneer.* Illustrated with the paintings and drawings of E. A. Wilson. Philadelphia: J. B. Lippincott, 1970.

Bölsche, Wilhelm. *Haeckel: His Life and Work.* Philadelphia: Jacobs, 1906.

Bown, Stephen R. *Scurvy: How a Surgeon, a Mariner, and a Gentleman Solved the Greatest Medical Mystery of the Age of Sail.* New York: St. Martin's Press, 2004.

Campbell, Victor, and H. G. R. King. *The Wicked Mate: The Antarctic Diary of Victor Campbell.* Harleston, U.K.: Erskine Press, 1988.

Carpenter, Kenneth J. *The History of Scurvy and Vitamin C.* New York: Cambridge University Press, 1986.

Cherry-Garrard, Apsley. *The Worst Journey in the World: Antarctic 1910–1913, with Panoramas, Maps, and Illustrations by the Late Doctor Edward A. Wilson and Other Members of the Expedition, in Two Volumes.* London: Constable and Co., 1922 (available online at www.gutenberg.org/etext/14363).

———. *The Worst Journey in the World: Antarctic 1910–1913 with Maps and Illustrations by the Late Doctor Edward A. Wilson and Other Members of the Expedition, One Volume Edition.* London: Chatto & Windus, 1937.

———. *The Worst Journey in the World: Antarctic 1910–1913.* Introduction by Caroline Alexander. New York: Penguin, 2006.

Debenham, Frank. *In the Antarctic: Stories of Scott's Last Expedition.* London: J. Murray, 1952.

——. *The Quiet Land: The Diaries of Frank Debenham, Member of the British-Antarctic Expedition, 1910–1913*. Harleston, U.K.: Erskine Press, 1992.

Fairfax, Ferdinand (director). *The Last Place on Earth*. BSF Entertainment, Richmond, Ontario, 1985. Film.

Fiennes, Sir Ranulph. *Mind over Matter: The Epic Crossing of the Antarctic Continent*. New York: Delacorte Press, 1993.

——. *Beyond the Limits: The Lessons Learned from a Lifetime's Adventures*. London: Little, Brown, 2000.

——. *Race to the Pole: Tragedy, Heroism, and Scott's Antarctic Quest*. New York: Hyperion, 2004. Originally published as *Captain Scott*. London: Hodder & Stoughton, 2003.

Frend, Charles (director). *Scott of the Antarctic*. 1948. Ealing Studios, London. Film.

Freedman, Bernard J. "Dr. Edward Wilson of the Antarctic: A Biographical Sketch, Followed by an Inquiry into the Nature of His Last Illness." *Proceedings of the Royal Society of Medicine* 47 (1953).

Gould, Stephen Jay. *Ontogeny and Phylogeny*. Cambridge, Mass.: Harvard University Press, Belknap Press, 1977.

Gran, Tryggve. *The Norwegian with Scott: Tryggve Gran's Antarctic Diary, 1910–1913*. Edited by Geoffrey Hattersley-Smith. Translated by Ellen Johanne McGhie. Greenwich, U.K.: National Maritime Museum, 1984.

Harvie, David I. *Limeys: The True Story of One Man's War Against Ignorance, the Establishment and the Deadly Scurvy*. Stroud, U.K.: Sutton, 2002.

Hemming, John. *Atlas of Exploration*. New York: Oxford University Press, 1997.

Huler, Scott. *Defining the Wind: The Beaufort Scale, and How a*

Nineteenth-Century Admiral Turned Science into Poetry. New York: Crown, 2004.

Huntford, Roland. *Scott and Amundsen.* New York: Putnam, 1980.

Hurley, Frank. *Argonauts of the South.* New York: G. P. Putnam's Sons, 1925.

Huxley, Elspeth. *Scott of the Antarctic.* New York: Atheneum, 1978.

Jones, A. G. E. *Antarctica Observed: Who Discovered the Antarctic Continent?* Whitby, U.K.: Caedmon of Whitby, 1982.

Jones, Max. *The Last Great Quest: Captain Scott's Antarctic Sacrifice.* New York: Oxford University Press, 2003.

Lambert, Katherine. *Hell with a Capital H: An Epic Story of Antarctic Survival.* London: Pimlico, 2002.

Lansing, Alfred. *Endurance: Shackleton's Incredible Voyage.* New York: McGraw-Hill, 1959.

Lashly, William. *Under Scott's Command: Lashly's Antarctic Diaries.* New York: Taplinger, 1969.

McElrea, Richard, and David L. Harrowfield. *Polar Castaways: The Ross Sea Party of Sir Ernest Shackleton, 1914–17.* Montreal: McGill-Queen's University Press, 2004.

Markham, Sir Clements R. *Antarctic Obsession: A Personal Narrative of the Origins of the British National Antarctic Expedition, 1901–1904.* Harleston, U.K.: Erskine Press, 1986.

Mear, Roger, and Robert Swan. *A Walk to the Pole: To the Heart of Antarctica in the Footsteps of Scott.* New York: Crown, 1987.

Mountevans, Edward Ratcliffe Garth Russell, Baron Evans. *South with Scott.* London: W. Collins Sons, 1921.

——. *The Antarctic Challenged.* New York: Grove Press, 1957.

Mountfield, David. *A History of Polar Exploration.* New York: Dial Press, 1974.

Muller-Schwarze, Dietland, and Christine Muller-Schwarze. "Wilson's Stone Hut at Cape Crozier." *Antarctic Journal*, January–February 1972.

Nansen, Fridtjof. *The First Crossing of Greenland*. London and New York: Longmans, Green, 1890.

Neider, Charles. *Antarctica: Authentic Accounts of Life and Exploration in the World's Highest, Driest, Windiest, Coldest and Most Remote Continent*. New York: Random House, 1972.

———. *Edge of the World, Ross Island, Antarctica: A Personal and Historical Narrative*. Garden City, N.Y.: Doubleday, 1974.

Ponting, Herbert George. *The Great White South; or, With Scott in the Antarctic: Being an Account of Experiences with Captain Scott's South Pole Expedition and of the Nature Life of the Antarctic*. New York: R. M. McBride & Co., 1923.

———. *Another World: Photographs in the United States, Asia, Europe and Antarctica, 1900–1912*. London: Sidgwick & Jackson, 1975.

———. *90° South*. Released 1933. New York: Milestone Film & Video, 1992. Film.

Ponting, Herbert George, and Ann Savours. *Scott's Last Voyage, Through the Antarctic Camera of Herbert Ponting*. New York: Praeger, 1975.

Preston, Diana. *A First Rate Tragedy: Robert Falcon Scott and the Race to the South Pole*. Boston: Houghton Mifflin, 1998.

Roscoe, John Hobbie. *Antarctica, Aerial Photographic Coverage*. Washington, D.C.: U.S. Navy, 1950.

Rowell, Galen A. *Poles Apart: Parallel Visions of the Arctic and Antarctic*. Berkeley: University of California Press, 1995.

Sale, Richard. *Polar Reaches: The History of Arctic and Antarctic Exploration*. Seattle: Mountaineers Books, 2002.

Savours, Ann. *The Voyages of the Discovery: The Illustrated History of Scott's Ship*. London: Virgin, 1992.

Scott, Robert Falcon. *The Voyage of the Discovery*. London: Smith, Elder, 1905.

———. *Scott's Last Expedition . . . Vol. I Being the Journals of Captain R. F. Scott, R.N., C.V.O.; Vol. II Being the Reports of the Journeys and the Scientific Work Undertaken by Dr. E. A. Wilson and the Surviving Members of the Expedition*. London: Smith, Elder, 1913.

———. *Journals: Captain Scott's Last Expedition*. Edited by Max Jones. New York: Oxford University Press, 2005.

Seaver, George. *Edward Wilson: Nature-Lover*. New York: E. P. Dutton, 1938.

———. *"Birdie" Bowers of the Antarctic*. London: J. Murray, 1938.

———. *Edward Wilson of the Antarctic: Naturalist and Friend: Together with a Memoir of Oriana Wilson*. London: J. Murray, 1948.

———. *The Faith of Edward Wilson*. London: J. Murray, 1957.

Shackleton, Sir Ernest Henry. *The Heart of the Antarctic: Being the Story of the British Antarctic Expedition 1907–1909*. London: William Heinemann, 1909.

———. *South: The Story of Shackleton's Last Expedition, 1914–1917*. New York: Macmillan, 1920.

Smith, Michael. *Tom Crean: Unsung Hero of the Scott and Shackleton Antarctic Expeditions*. Seattle: Mountaineers Books, 2001.

———. *I Am Just Going Outside: Captain Oates—Antarctic Tragedy*. Staplehurst, U.K.: Spellmount, 2002.

Solomon, Susan. *The Coldest March: Scott's Fatal Antarctic Expedition*. New Haven: Yale University Press, 2001.

Spufford, Francis. *I May Be Some Time: Ice and the English Imagination*. New York: St. Martin's Press, 1997.

Sturridge, Charles (director). *Shackleton*. A&E Video, New York, 2002. Film.

Taylor, Thomas Griffith. *With Scott: The Silver Lining*. London: Smith, Elder, 1916.

———. *Antarctic Adventure and Research*. New York and London: D. Appleton and Co., 1930.

Thomson, David. *Scott's Men*. New York: Thunder's Mouth Press, 2002.

———. *Scott, Shackleton, and Amundsen: Ambition and Tragedy in the Antarctic*. New York: Thunder's Mouth Press, 2002.

Wheeler, Sara. *Terra Incognita: Travels in Antarctica*. New York: Random House, 1998.

———. *Cherry: A Life of Apsley Cherry-Garrard*. New York: Random House, 2002.

Willis, Clint. *Ice: Stories of Survival from Polar Exploration*. New York: Thunder's Mouth Press, 1999.

Wilson, D. M., and D. B. Elder. *Cheltenham in Antarctica: The Life of Edward Wilson* (Walkabout Series). Cheltenham, U.K.: Reardon, 2000.

Wilson, Edward Adrian. *Diary of the "Discovery" Expedition to the Antarctic Regions 1901–1904*. London: Blandford Press, 1966.

———. *Edward Wilson's Birds of the Antarctic*. London: Blandford Press, 1967.

———. *Diary of the "Terra Nova" Expedition to the Antarctic,*

1910–1912: An Account of Scott's Last Expedition. London: Blandford Press, 1972.

———. *Edward Wilson's Nature Notebooks.* Cheltenham, U.K.: Reardon, 2004.

Wright, Charles S. *Silas: The Antarctic Diaries and Memoir of Charles S. Wright.* Columbus: Ohio State University Press, 1993.

Yelverton, David. *Antarctica Unveiled: Scott's Last Expedition and the Quest for the Unknown Continent.* Boulder: University Press of Colorado, 2000.

ILLUSTRATION CREDITS

ATL	Used with permission of the Alexander Turnbull Library, Wellington, New Zealand
EJH	Map adapted from version redrawn by E. J. Hatch after Apsley Cherry-Garrard's original design, from *The Worst Journey in the World: Antarctic 1910–1913* by Apsley Cherry-Garrard (London: Chatto & Windus, 1965)
EW	Edward Wilson
HP	Herbert Ponting
LC	Used with permission of The Lordprice Collection, New Malden, Surrey, England
RGS	Used with permission of the Royal Geographical Society, London, England
SPRI	Used with permission of the Scott Polar Research Institute, University of Cambridge, Cambridge, England
WJ 1937	From *The Worst Journey in the World: Antarctic 1910–1913* by Apsley Cherry-Garrard (London: Chatto & Windus, 1937)

WJ Gutenberg   From Project Gutenberg's online edition of *The Worst Journey in the World: Antarctic 1910–1913* by Apsley Cherry-Garrard, http://www.gutenberg.org/files/14363/14363-h/index.htm#

(page ii) HP, "Sledger at the Foot of Glacier and Mount Erebus," 1912, RGS. (xii) HP, "A. Cherry-Garrard," 1911, RGS. (2) Anonymous, "Second Torpid," 1906, used with permission of the Governing Body of Christ Church, Oxford, England. (5) John Thomson, "Robert Falcon Scott," ca. 1911, ATL. (8) HP, "Dr. Wilson Standing at Door of Hut," 1911, RGS. (11) EW, "Emperor Penguin, Moulting. Lady Newnes' Bay," 1902, SPRI. (15) HP, "The *Terra Nova*," 1910–13, RGS. (16) *Terra Nova* expedition logo, SPRI. (20) HP, "The *Terra Nova* in Heavy Weather," 1910?, RGS. (25) EJH, SPRI. (27) HP, "Captain Lawrence Edward Grace Oates and Ponies, Antarctica," 1911, ATL. (29) HP, "Husky Osman," 1910–12, RGS. (31) HP, "At the Pump on the *Terra Nova*," 1910, SPRI. (34) HP, "Portrait of Lieut. Bowers," 1911, RGS. (36) Advertisement for Oxo beef bouillon, 1913, LC. (40) HP, "The *Terra Nova* Held Up in the Pack," 1910, RGS. (41) HP, Cinematographing the *Terra Nova*'s Bow Forcing Aside the Floes," 1910, RGS. (42) Film poster for the Gaumont Co. Ltd., 1912?, ATL. (45a) HP, "Dr. Wilson Shooting from the *Terra Nova*," 1910?, RGS. (45b) EW, "Sea Leopard Chasing an Emperor Penguin Underwater," 1901–04, SPRI. (48) HP, "Group of All the Shore Party, Except Clissold (Laid Up) and Ponting (Photoing)," 1911, RGS. (51) C. S. Wright, "The Barrier Pressure at Cape Crozier, with the Knoll," *WJ* 1937. (54) HP, "Officers Hauling Sledges of Fodder from the *Terra Nova* to Cape Evans," 1911, RGS. (55) HP, "Camp near Erebus, Antarctica," 1911, ATL. (58) HP, "Grotto in an Iceberg," 1911, ATL. (60) HP, "Taking the Ill-Fated Motor-Sledge off the *Terra Nova*, Antarctica," 1911, ATL. (61)

HP, "Hut, Bergs, and Clouds," 1911, RGS. (63) HP, "Captain Scott and the Southern Party," 1911, ATL. (64) EJH, SPRI. (67) HP, "A Whale Diving Under Ice," 1910–12, RGS. (68) HP, "Thomas Clissold Making Bread," 1911, ATL. (70) HP, "Cherry-Garrard at His Typewriter, Antarctica," 1911, ATL. (71) HP, "Bunk Beds, Antarctica," 1911, ATL. (72) HP, "Henry Robertson Bowers, Dr. Wilson, and Apsley George Benet Cherry-Garrard Before Leaving for Cape Crozier, Antarctica," 1911, ATL. (75) Nicola Perscheid, "Ernst H.P.A. Haeckel," 1904, the National Library of Medicine, Bethesda, Maryland. (81) EW, Midwinter dinner menu, 1911, SPRI. (84–85) EJH, SPRI. (86) EW, "Camping After Dark (detail)," date unknown, *WJ* 1937. (87) HP, "Dr. Atkinson's Frostbitten Hand," 1911, RGS. (91) HP, "Finnesko (Boots)," 1912, RGS. (99) HP, "Thomas Crean and Petty Officer Evans Mending Sleeping Bags, Antarctica," 1911, ATL. (104) HP, "Emperor Penguin's Eggs," 1912, RGS. (106) EW, "Cape Crozier and Its Neighbourhood, Drawn from Memory," ca. 1910, SPRI. (111) EW, "The Emperor Penguins Nursing Their Chicks on the Sea-Ice, with the Cliffs of the Barrier Behind," date unknown, *WJ* 1937. (116) EW, "Pencil Sketch in the Draft Report of the Winter Journey from Cape Evans to Cape Crozier," 1911, SPRI. (122) EW, "Hold Fast," date unknown, SPRI. (129) EW, "Down a Crevasse," date unknown, *WJ* 1937. (134) HP, "Dr. Wilson, Henry Robertson Bowers, and Apsley George Benet Cherry-Garrard, Antarctica," 1911, ATL. (136) Henry Robertson Bowers, "Leaving the 3 Degree Depot," date unknown, ATL. (139) HP, "Robert Falcon Scott in His Den, Antarctica," 1911, ATL. (141) EJH, SPRI. (142–43) Robert Falcon Scott, "Ponies Pulling Sleds in the Antarctic," 1911, ATL. (145) EW, "Camp on the Barrier. 22 November 1911," *WJ* Gutenberg. (146) Robert Falcon Scott, "Men on Beardmore Glacier Pulling a Sled Laden with Supplies," 1911, ATL. (148a) HP, "C. S. Wright on Return from Barrier," 1912, RGS. (148b) HP, "Dr. Atkinson,"

1911, RGS. (149a) HP, "A. C. Cherry-Garrard on Return from Barrier," 1912, RGS. (149b) HP, "P. Keohane on Return from the Barrier," 1912, RGS. (150) C. S. Wright, "Our Night Camp at the Foot of the Buckley Island Icefalls," 1911, *WJ* Gutenberg. (152a) Anonymous, "William Lashly Standing by a Wolseley Motor Sleigh," 1911, ATL. (152b) HP, "Seaman Crean," date unknown, RGS. (153) HP, "Lieut. Evans at Glacier Tongue," 1911, RGS. (155) Robert Falcon Scott, "View of the Camp at 1 Ton Depot, Antarctica," 1911, ATL. (157a) HP, "Petty Officer Evans," 1911, RGS. (157b) HP, "Captain Lawrence Edward Grace Oates," ca. 1911, ATL. (159) Henry Robertson Bowers, "The Pole Party at the Norwegian Tent, Antarctica," 1912, ATL. (160) Henry Robertson Bowers, "At the South Pole," 1912, ATL. (163) F. Debenham, "The Dog Party Leaves Hut Point," 1912, *WJ* Gutenberg. (166) *The Daily Mirror*, 21 May 1913, LC. (168) Anonymous, "Roald Amundsen in Polar Kit," 1911, LC. (170) Anonymous, "Oscar Wisting at the Pole," 1911, LC. (172) HP, "Captain Scott on Ski," 1911, RGS. (176) F. Debenham, "Krisravitza," date unknown, *WJ* Gutenberg. (179) EW, "Cape Evans in Winter, Looking Northwards from Under the Ramp," date unknown, *WJ* Gutenberg. (182) HP, "An Emperor Penguin," 1910–12, RGS. (184) Anonymous, "In Memoriam," 1913, National Library of Australia, Canberra, Australia.